50 DAYS OF PRAYER

Oregon Coast

For the Church,

MY Community

State Nation World

LINDA HANRATTY

50 DAYS OF PRAYER

Oregon Coast

By Linda Hanratty

www.50dop.org

© 2020 Tillamook Countywide Prayer Team.

All rights reserved.

Contributing Authors: Cami Aufdermauer, Sandy Blaser, Terry Blaser, Peter Carlson, Pastor Doug Edwards, Lynn Ferder, Donald Foery, Linda Hanratty, Mike Hanratty, George Hodgdon, Ray Hopfer, Pastor Marv Kasemeier, Pastor Jim Moore, Carrie Werner

Edited by: Ray Hopfer, Linda Hanratty and Terry Blaser

Cover Design by: Ray Hopfer

Published by: 50 Days of Prayer
1000 Main Street, Suite 12
Tillamook, OR 97141

For current information about using this book/contact info see www.50dop.org

e-book   ISBN 978-1-952515-01-9
paperback   ISBN 978-1-952515-00-2

Custom Editions avail for your state/county/group/area 50dop.org/custom (See **Forward** page for more info – web site will have the most current)

We invite YOU to make a difference!

In Just 10 Minutes a day…join thousands as we lift up a prayer shield over:

YOUR CHURCH
YOUR COMMUNITY
YOUR STATE
YOUR NATION
YOUR WORLD

The World that God LOVES!

Add YOUR Prayer Shield of faith over our land

TABLE OF CONTENTS

Days 31-40   For OUR NATION

Days 41-50   For THE WORLD

Forward

You can use this book by yourself, but it is often used by communities for specific prayer campaigns for 50 days. Communities are encouraged to use a prayer guide that contains info to go with many of the 50 days such as statistics or the names of office holders so that your prayers can be more specific for each day.

We can provide your team with a **template** and instructions so that you can provide a **reading guide** for everyone who is participating in your 50 days of prayer campaign.

We can even produce a **custom book** and **reading guide** for your community if you like. You can find out how to do this at our web site 50dop.org/custom. You are encouraged to share this book and information on how a community can use it for concentrated periods of prayer with any prayer leaders that you know.

Terry Blaser
50 Days of Prayer
Tillamook, Oregon
50dop.org/contact

Introduction:

In 2013, the Tillamook County Wide Prayer Team published its first 40 Days of Prayer in an effort to build unity within the Body of Christ. Since then, we have invited churches in our county and state to join this prayer effort with a new book most years. Every year three-fourths of the churches that span our 75-mile-long county, join together to agree in prayer. We are seeing amazing answers to prayer!

In 2016, the first edition of *50 Days of Prayer*, was published and distributed. It has been written by 14 Christian authors. You will notice different personalities and passion arise in each prayer. Some are prayer leaders, and some are pastors. We asked our authors from around the state to incorporate the scripture into each prayer. What you have before you is a powerful tool that will lead you to pray for topics that impact you but likely, you never thought to pray for. The Word does not return void but accomplishes that for which He sent it! (Isaiah 55:11). You will see the paraphrased Word woven throughout this book, so BELIEVE that your prayer will make a difference, because it will! This is very exciting!

This book, if it is distributed by your church should come with a "50 Days of Prayer, **Reading Guide**," containing a daily reading schedule, statistics for your community, county, state, nation and world as well as the names of your leaders. This can be updated annually. Please take the time to open the Reading Guide and lift up the names of your leaders and sense the weight of the statistics. Please use it all year long!

In 2019, we felt the Lord was calling us to enlarge the prayer territory. Our 50 Days of Prayer Team began to work with Pray Oregon to build a "Prayer Shield" over Oregon and the Nation. The goal is that on the first of every month more Counties will begin 50 Days of Prayer. This raises a continuous prayer shield over our state and nation all year long! As new communities are added, eventually every state will be bathed in continuous prayer. This prayer can spread like wildfire... the fire of God to bring healing to our people and nation. If each church catches the fire of His love to lift up passionate prayer over our people and land, we can expect a sweeping move of God. So, let's do it! Give 10 minutes to bring yourself and your family to God's throne of grace to find help for our people. Use this book as a launch pad to pray what God puts on your heart. Go for it! And thank you for praying!

Linda Hanratty, President of Tillamook County Wide Prayer Team

Isaiah 58:6-12 "Is this not the fast that I have chosen:

To loose the bonds of wickedness,

To undo the heavy burdens,

To let the oppressed go free,

And that you break every yoke?

^{7} Is it not to share your bread with the hungry,

And that you bring to your house the poor who are cast out;

When you see the naked, that you cover him,

And not hide yourself from your own flesh?

^{8} Then your light shall break forth like the morning,

Your healing shall spring forth speedily,

And your righteousness shall go before you;

The glory of the Lord shall be your rear guard.

^{9} Then you shall call, and the Lord will answer;

You shall cry, and He will say, 'Here I am.'

"If you take away the yoke from your midst,

The pointing of the finger, and speaking wickedness,

^{10} If you extend your soul to the hungry

And satisfy the afflicted soul,

Then your light shall dawn in the darkness,

And your darkness shall be as the noonday.

^{11} The Lord will guide you continually,

And satisfy your soul in drought,

And strengthen your bones;

You shall be like a watered garden,

And like a spring of water, whose waters do not fail.

^{12} Those from among you

Shall build the old waste places;

You shall raise up the foundations of many generations;

And you shall be called the Repairer of the Breach,

The Restorer of Streets to Dwell In.

10 Days for the Church

Day 1   Repentance

Joel 2:12-13   Now, therefore, says the LORD, Turn to Me with all your heart, with fasting, with weeping, and with mourning. So rend your heart, and not your garments; return to the LORD your God, for He is gracious and merciful, slow to anger, and of great kindness; and He relents from doing harm.

Romans 2:4   Or do you despise the riches of His goodness, forbearance, and longsuffering, not knowing that the goodness of God leads you to repentance?

Hosea 6:1-3, 6; 2 Corinthians 7:9,10

PRAYER:

Father God, we acknowledge that You are holy and righteous, so we come and bow our hearts before You. We praise You that You are compassionate and have given us access to come before Your throne. It is Your kindness that draws us to repentance as Your Word declares, so we thank You for extending Your loving-kindness to us today. Allow us to see our sin for what it is and be sorrowful for it, because it separates us from You and cost the life of Your only begotten Son. We pray this not only for ourselves, but for our nation. O God, how we have offended You. We repent on behalf of our nation, our leaders and citizens alike. May we recognize our offenses and turn away from them to You who are willing to forgive and restore. May we walk in humility and gratitude and perform deeds appropriate to repentance.

Father, thank You for Your grace and mercy which is provided new for us today.

*Because of Your grace, I ask You to forgive me for any way that I have grieved You or Your Holy Spirit. Help me to hear Your voice as I bring to mind these things. Forgive me, Father, for I have sinned against You and my people in the following ways..._____ (listen and obey!). I ask You to cleanse me from this unrighteousness and renew a right spirit within me. Show me how to respond in my world to make this attitude and my relationships right. It is in the all-powerful name of Jesus our Lord and Savior we pray. Amen.

Day 2   Praise and Thanksgiving

Psalm 100:1-5   Make a joyful shout to the LORD, all you lands! Serve the LORD with gladness; Come before His presence with singing. Know that the LORD, He is God; It is He who has made us, and not we ourselves; We are His people and the sheep of His pasture. Enter into His gates with thanksgiving, And into His courts with praise. Be thankful to Him, and bless His name. For the LORD is good; His mercy is everlasting, And His truth endures to all generations.

Ephesians 1:3,6   Blessed be the God and Father of our Lord Jesus Christ, who has blessed us with every spiritual blessing in heavenly places ...to the praise of the glory of His grace, by which He made us accepted in the Beloved.

Psalm 103; Ephesians 1:3-11

PRAYER:

Lord God, we lift our hearts in thanksgiving and praise to You, for You are God alone and worthy of all praise. We bless Your name for You are good. You are the One who made us; we are Yours and therefore live for You. May our lips speak great joy and our service be given with gladness. Hear the joyful songs of our hearts that honor You as we meditate on Your everlasting lovingkindness and faithfulness to every generation. When we are weighed down by the burdens of sin and the cares of this life, draw our hearts back to You. Lift our eyes to see Your glory that we may praise You in a way that is worthy of Your name. We are so blessed by Your marvelous, amazing grace! May our lives show our gratitude for each of these blessings that are ours in abundance.

*And now, Lord, I thank You for the many blessings in my life! _____ (name them!) Fill my heart with thankfulness every day, that brings glory to You! Lord Jesus I live to praise the glory of Your grace! Amen

Day 3   Attitudes and Actions

Proverbs 3:5-8   *Trust in the LORD with all your heart, and lean not on your own understanding; In all your ways acknowledge Him, and He shall direct your paths. Do not be wise in your own eyes; Fear the LORD and depart from evil. It will be health to your flesh, and strength to your bones.*

Hebrews 12:1-3   *Therefore we also, since we are surrounded by so great a cloud of witnesses, let us lay aside every weight, and the sin which so easily ensnares us, and let us run with endurance the race that is set before us, looking unto Jesus, the author and finisher of our faith, who for the joy that was set before Him endured the cross, despising the shame, and has sat down at the right hand of the throne of God. For consider Him who endured such hostility from sinners against Himself, lest you become weary and discouraged in your souls.*

Philippians 2:3-16

PRAYER:

Lord, You call us in Your Word to "Do nothing from selfishness or empty conceit, but with humility of mind regard one another as more important than (our)selves" and to "not merely look out for (our) own personal interests, but also for the interests of others." Then You call us up to the highest example: "Have this attitude in yourselves which was also in Christ Jesus," and highlight His humility in becoming a man and being obedient even to the point of dying on the cross. All of our sinful attitudes seem so petty in comparison.

*Forgive me Lord for taking Your sacrifice so lightly, and for all of the things I have done that put myself before You. Help me keep my eyes on You so that not only what I do, but what I say, and think will be in gratitude for Your great sacrifice that purchased my redemption. Lord, bring to mind the areas of my life that distract me. _____ (Listen, repent and obey). Strengthen me, Lord, so that I will not give in to the temptations that would ensnare me. Set me free from the bondage of wrong attitudes and actions so that I may not just walk, but "run with endurance the race that is set before me, looking to You, the author and finisher of my faith." In the name of Jesus, our living Savior, I pray. Amen.

Day 4   Salvation through Christ

John 1:12-13   But as many as received Him, to them He gave the right to become children of God, to those who believe in His name: who were born, not of blood, nor of the will of the flesh, nor of the will of man, but of God.

John 17:3   And this is eternal life, that they may know You, the only true God, and Jesus Christ whom You have sent.

John 3:16-18; Romans 10:8-13; 2 Peter 1:2-8

PRAYER:

Father in heaven, I thank You that by receiving You I have been given the right to be Your child. It is by Your will and no other that we are born again to eternal life through believing in Your name and who You are: Creator, Redeemer, Savior, Lord, God. Thank You, Father, for providing everything I need to have eternal life: to know You, the only true God, and Jesus Christ, Your only begotten Son, whom You sent to be our Savior. Thank you, Jesus for coming to show us the Father's love, and not only living a perfect life but being the perfect sacrifice to take away the sins of the whole world, including my sins. And not only did You die, but You were buried and raised up and exalted to the highest place at the right hand of the throne of God as Lord of all.

*As Lord of my life, Jesus, I yield to Your authority over every area of my life, and I submit to Your control. Show me areas in my life that I need to submit to you: _____ (listen and obey!) I repent and turn from all my sins and want to be obedient to all You have commanded. And as I do, I thank You, that You give me Your Spirit to empower me to do it. Live in me in the fullest way possible so that Your life may be seen in me and that others are drawn to know and trust You also. Use me Lord in Your Kingdom, however You choose. I am Yours. In the name of Jesus, I pray. Amen.

Day 5   Broken Relationships

Isaiah 58:11-12   The LORD will guide you continually, and satisfy your soul in drought, and strengthen your bones; You shall be like a watered garden, and like a spring of water, whose waters do not fail. Those from among you Shall build the old waste places; You shall raise up the foundations of many generations; and you shall be called the Repairer of the Breach, The Restorer of Streets to Dwell In.

Luke 15:11-32; Colossians 3:12-17

PRAYER:
Father God, You declare in Your Word a day in which Your people will "rebuild the ancient ruins...raise up the age-old foundations...be called the repairer of the breach, the restorer of the paths in which to dwell." Lord, we want to be those people! To do that, we need You to continually guide us and give strength so that we will be like a watered garden, and like a spring of water whose waters do not fail. For all those who have been wounded and fallen away, for those who have felt unloved and unappreciated, for all the offended and broken-hearted, Lord we pray for their healing and restoration. Give us wisdom and courage to lovingly help the healing process and restore relationships, bringing children back to safety in You. We pray for all the prodigal sons and daughters to return to You. Guard and guide them back home. Lord, Your Word says You "run" to receive them, when they are far off. Prepare us to receive them as You do; to love, encourage, and bless them with the Father's love.

*In Your kindness Lord, please show me any areas of offense, unloving attitudes and actions that have contributed to brokenness. Lead me to repent; forgive me; and give me grace to forgive and love as

You do. As You reveal anything in this regard, I am listening: _____ (listen and obey!) I want to be faithful in obedience to You. I pray for courage to do the right thing in Your love. In Jesus name, Amen.

Day 6   Entrapments of the Age

John 10:10 *The thief does not come except to steal, and to kill, and to destroy. I have come that they may have life, and that they may have it more abundantly.*

1 John 4:1-6; 2 Corinthians 10:4-5; Ephesians 6:10-20

PRAYER:

O Lord, our God, how great Thou art! When we look around us today, we see many counterfeits, impostors, and deceivers, all designed to destroy Your people and plan. Yet we know You are greater! Help us keep our eyes on You, then we can see the deceptions clearly for what they are. Expose the New Age Spirituality and Wiccan ideologies and all other false religions set up in opposition to Truth. Cause us to have a greater hunger and thirst for You and Your Word which alone can satisfy. May we be diligent like the Bereans and full of grace and truth like Jesus. You have equipped and empowered us with a whole arsenal; help us use it wisely and diligently, not shrinking back or losing ground. Your TRUTH prepares us for what is to come, Your RIGHTEOUSNESS envelopes us with protection, Your GOSPEL OF PEACE is that upon which we stand, our FAITH is a protective shield, Your SALVATION guards our minds, Your Word is our weapon when activated by Your Spirit, and PRAYER our engagement in the battle. Lord, keep us alert and persevering that Your Word will go forth and prevail.

*Lord God, I ask that You expose the lies, the subtle schemes of the enemy that have crept into my life. _____ (Listen and obey!) Forgive me for participation in anything of the darkness; search my heart for any deception. Cleanse me from all unrighteousness. Do this also for the Church. We thank You and praise You, in the name of Jesus our Lord, Amen.

Day 7   Strongholds in Our Land

Jeremiah 29:11 *For I know the thoughts that I think toward you, says the Lord, thoughts of peace, and not of evil, to give you a hope and a future.*

John 10:10 ... *I have come that they may have life, and that they may have it more abundantly.*

PRAYER:

Father, we come to You in the mighty name of Jesus Christ, King of kings and Lord of lords. We give You praise, honor and glory today for Your grace and mercy toward Your children who have given up hope for their lives and futures. Today we stand in the gap for those who are contemplating ending their lives because they cannot bear the heaviness and pain. We lift up those whose lives have been devastated by drugs or alcohol. We cry out for those in deep suffering who have had abortions or are contemplating abortion. Hear the cries of the lost and of the lives stolen. Father, there are deep wounds in our County from hatred and prejudice. Heal the despair that has occurred here, the injustice done to the Native Americans, African Americans, Hispanics and others of different racial origins. Where there is still hidden wickedness, we ask You, Lord to uncover it so that it can be dealt with.

Father, You said, "For I know the thoughts that I think toward you, thoughts of peace, and not of evil, to give you a hope and a future," but the enemy has come in to kill, steal and destroy those hopes by clouding their minds with hopeless, negative thoughts. Darkness has clouded their eyes, so their hearts are weighed down with heaviness and confusion. But You have said, "I am come that they might have life, and that they might have it more abundantly."

We declare Your Word that says, "Let the wicked forsake his way and the unrighteous man his thoughts, and let him return unto the Lord, and to our God, and He will abundantly pardon." Where the enemy has come in, like a flood the Spirit of the Lord will lift up a standard against him! We see Your water rising Lord! Healing waters, floods upon the dry ground! The earth shall be filled with the knowledge of the glory of the Lord as the waters cover the sea! Let You glory cover this land!

Father, You have said to Arise, Shine, for thy light is come, and the glory of the Lord is risen upon thee. For, behold the darkness shall cover the earth, and gross darkness the people: but the Lord shall arise upon thee, and His glory shall be seen upon thee. Where there has been darkness, depression, addiction, hopelessness and confusion, we say LET THERE BE LIGHT! Father, remove the veil, the covering over these people, command Your Light to shine in their darkness! We call forth the Church to ARISE and SHINE in our County. We stand and cry out for Your mercy and healing. We join together in one accord and bind the works of darkness over these people in Jesus' name and decree and declare LIFE over our land! We declare open heavens over in this place!

Father, arise in the hearts of Your people! Your love is the key! Fill us with Your Spirit! Give us beauty for ashes, the oil of joy for mourning, the garment of praise for the spirit of heaviness, that we in this County might be called trees of righteousness, the planting of the Lord, that You might be glorified! In Jesus Name! Amen!

Day 8   The Church

Hebrews 10:23-25 *Let us hold fast the confession of our hope with-out wavering, for He who promised is faithful. And let us consider one another in order to stir up love and good works, not forsaking the assembling of ourselves together, as is the manner of some, but ex-horting one another, and so much the more as you see the Day ap-proaching.*

1 Peter 4:10-11 *As each one has received a gift, minister it to one another, as good stewards of the manifold grace of God. If anyone speaks, let him speak as the oracles of God. If anyone ministers, let him do it as with the ability which God supplies, that in all things God may be glorified through Jesus Christ, to whom belong the glory and the dominion forever and ever. Amen.*

1 Corinthians 3:5-11

PRAYER:

Lord Jesus, Your Word tells us not to forsake the assembling of Your people. We need this to strengthen our relationships with You and each other, to teach and be accountable to Your Word. You have called me to be an important part of Your church in my community. You have given each of us gifts to use in service to the Body of which we are a part, and You expect us to use them faithfully as we grow to become more like You. Thank You for the privilege to have an im-portant part in Your Kingdom! May the churches of this county be filled with loving, faithful servants who are filled with Your Spirit, doing the work of the ministry, as You have commissioned us to do. May the truth of Your Word be proclaimed with power; the life-changing power of Your gospel. May we be faithful in doing our part

- sowing seeds, watering, whatever You have called us to do- and give You all the glory for the growth that You bring-- in my life, in my church, in my community. In Your name I pray. Amen.

*Lord, make me an instrument of Your peace in my church and my community, loving and serving with all my heart. Thank You for giving me responsibility for what You have called me to do. (Forgive me when I have been judgmental or when I have held back). Give me boldness to step out of my "comfort box" to help love others into Your Kingdom. Make me sensitive to hearing Your voice and may I be quick to respond to Your nudge. Lord, are You nudging me right now? I am listening! _____ (listen and obey!). In Jesus Name. Amen!

I pray for the churches in my community_____.

Day 9   Relationships and Unity

Psalm 133:1-3   Behold, how good and how pleasant it is for brethren to dwell together in unity! It is like the precious oil upon the head, running down on the beard, the beard of Aaron, Running down on the edge of his garments. It is like the dew of Hermon, descending upon the mountains of Zion; For there the LORD commanded the blessing— Life forevermore.

John 14:20   At that day you will know that I am in My Father, and you in Me, and I in you.

John 17; 1 Corinthians 12:18-27

PRAYER:

Father God. You have described Your relationship between Yourself, Jesus, and the Holy Spirit as being ONE. You have called the Church, although we are many parts, to be as One, even as You God, are One. You are the Head and we are the Body. Forgive us Lord for any wrong thinking, anything other than the mind of Christ, toward any other part of the Body, thinking more highly of ourselves than we ought to think. Help us to love the rest of the parts of the Body, giving honor to one another, having the same care for one another. Even as You prayed Lord Jesus, when we Your people are united in love, the world will know the truth of who You are. Unite our hearts even as we are joined to You. In Jesus' name we pray for Your Church in our County _____ . I pray for the churches in my city _____ .

*And now, Lord, I ask You to reveal to my heart, areas of disunity that I have hung on to _____ (in my marriage, family, church, workplace, anywhere). Lord, forgive me where my thoughts and words have caused harm to others and to myself. Renew a right spirit of unity within me. Tell me what I must do to make things right: _____(listen and obey!). In Jesus Name. Amen!

Day 10   Pastors and Leaders

Ephesians 6:18-20   ...praying always with all prayer and supplication in the Spirit, being watchful to this end with all perseverance and supplication for all the saints *— and for me, that utterance may be given to me, that I may open my mouth boldly to make known the mystery of the gospel, or which I am an ambassador in chains; that in it I may speak boldly, as I ought to speak.*

Colossians 4:2-4   Continue earnestly in prayer, being vigilant in it with thanksgiving; meanwhile praying also for us, that God would open to us a door for the word, to speak the mystery of Christ, for which I am also in chains, that I may make it manifest, as I ought to speak.

1 Thessalonians 5:11-22

PRAYER:

Father God, we lift up all the saints who serve in Your Kingdom, especially those who labor in the preaching and teaching of Your Word. May all those committed to serve You in leadership roles in Your church be empowered by Your Holy Spirit to speak with boldness the truths of Your Gospel. Grant them clarity of mind and purity of heart to speak the truth in love, without reservation. May we, as Your people, find practical ways to demonstrate our love and support so that we may live in peace and Your Word be demonstrated in power.

*Lord, I pray for my pastor, _____, the Elders_____ and all the leaders who teach and minister to me. I thank You for each one of them. Help me to lift them up to You in prayer, and bless them in their ministry, their homes, and give them God -inspired ability to serve. Lord, speak to my heart to know how to encourage and serve

our leaders. _____ (listen and obey!) Through Jesus Christ our Lord
we pray, Amen.

10 Days for My Community

Day 11   Our County Leaders and Government

1 Timothy 2:1-2   Therefore I exhort first of all that supplications, prayers, intercessions, and giving of thanks be made for all men, for kings and all who are in authority, that we may lead a quiet and peaceable life in all godliness and reverence.

Psalm 118:24, 25   This is the day which the Lord has made; We will rejoice and be glad in it. Save now, I pray O Lord; O Lord I pray, send now prosperity!

Proverbs 1:2-5

PRAYER:

Lord, we lift up those who are in positions of authority throughout this County, and all those who come alongside to provide for the day-to-day needs of our people. We pray blessing, wisdom, strength and divine guidance for them. Surround them with wise counsel. Give them ears to hear Your Holy Spirit guiding them into all truth. Give them great ideas and ability to lead our people. Help us as a people to express our gratitude and encouragement for their service.

- Thank the Lord for our public servants and for their families who support them.
- Pray for wisdom, discernment, health, protection and strength.
- Give them courage to stand for righteousness.

- We pray for resources and finances to meet every true need to perform their duties.

And now I pray for our County leaders by name and/or office _____.

In Jesus Name we pray! Amen

County Offices:

County Commissioners	Veteran's Services
County Clerk	Emergency Management
County Assessor	Victim's Assistance
County Treasurer	Planning Department
District Attorney	Road Department
Justice of the Peace	Juvenile Department
County Sheriff	All the others that you know of
County Surveyor	

Day 12   Our City Leaders and Government

Jeremiah 29:7   And seek the peace of the city where I have caused you to be carried away captive, and pray to the Lord for it; for in its peace you will have peace.

Isaiah 60:15   Whereas you have been forsaken and hated, so that no one went through you, I will make you an eternal excellence, a joy of many generations.

Isaiah 60:1-3, Matthew 5:14, Ezekiel 11:23, Isaiah 38:5-7

PRAYER:

Father, we honor You, and declare that You are Lord over my City of _____. We ask that a spirit of reverence and hope would come over my city as we honor You and that Your Spirit would spark the atmosphere with Your presence. We ask that You would pour out Your spirit of excellence and righteousness upon the leadership in my city, bringing blessing, vision and prosperity, and vigor to my community. Help us to love our city. Give us a heart to work to make it the place of restoration. Build up our walls, rebuild the ruins... Lord, we want to see our cities flourish in the courts of the Lord...restore and refresh us, Lord. Help us to testify to Your greatness. Let us be ready in season and out for the work that You have called us to do.

*Use me to make my city a better place to live... a place where Your glory dwells. Lord, direct me in how to do this: _____ (listen and obey!). In Jesus' Name we pray! Amen.

Now, I pray for the leaders in my City by name and/or office ____.

Day 13   Law Enforcement and Search & Rescue

Isaiah 60:17-18,21   *...I will also make your officers peace, and your magistrates righteousness. Violence shall no longer be heard in your land, neither wasting nor destruction within your borders; but you shall call your walls Salvation and your gates Praise. ...Also, your people shall all be righteous; they shall inherit the land forever, the branch of My planting, the work of My hands, that I may be glorified."*

Joshua 1:9   *Have I not commanded you? Be strong and of good courage; do not be afraid, nor be dismayed, for the Lord your God is with you wherever you go.*

John 15:13   *Greater love has no one than this, than to lay down one's life for his friends.*

Psalm 91, Isaiah 43:1-3, Psalm 23:4

PRAYER:

Father, we have come to appreciate the risks that our men and women who serve in law enforcement, fire and rescue, must face every day. They are motivated to serve and care for the land and people of their communities, facing unknown risks and circumstances for which they have diligently trained, and sometimes for things they lack experience and wisdom for that they must respond to. We as a community TRUST that they will show up! They do not know what the day will bring, what fears they will have to face, and the discouragement of dealing with difficult people all day long. They see life and death in its best and worst forms. These men and women need Your divinely inspired wisdom and ability to meet every circumstance, and they need protection over the things for which they have no control. The stress from these positions can cause high rates of "burn-out", sometimes corruption, and severe pressures on their marriages and families, so we ask that You would watch over our men and women who serve our community and beyond. Make them discerning and wise, strong and courageous, holy and righteous. Protect them in all their ways. Strengthen their families and marriages and let them not grow weary in well doing. Let them KNOW that You are with them.

*And now, I pray specifically for the officers and law enforcement agencies that serves my community _____.

In Jesus' Name we pray. Amen!

County Sheriff

County Corrections Facility

Parole and Probation

Search and Rescue

City Police Department

Youth Correctional Facility

State Police

County Chaplains

BLM

US Forest Service

County Courts, Judges, Juries

Day 14   Fire Departments

Psalm 66:12-13 *...We went through fire and through water; but You brought us out to rich fulfillment.*

Isaiah 43:2 *When you pass through the waters, I will be with you; and through the rivers, they shall not overflow you. When you walk through the fire, you shall not be burned, Nor shall the flame scorch you.*

PRAYER:

Father, we lift up the men and women who serve our county, fighting fires and serving our people in a multitude of ways. We pray a hedge of protection round about them.... And when they walk through the fire, it will not scorch them, because YOU, are in there with them. We ask for divine guidance and help as they risk their lives to help others. Your Word says that greater love has no man, than that he lay his life down for his friend. We pray great blessings over these volunteers and servants.

We pray that You would protect Our County and the whole region from the effects of forest fires. We ask Lord, that You would deflect every fiery dart, (cigarettes, campfires, arson, lightning), and cause them to fall as dust to the ground. Let the fire not light on our land. We praise You and thank You for Your loving care. We lift up the men and women of these fire departments and pray blessings over them and their families. We pray for those involved in Search and Rescue and Water Rescues. Help them to find those who are lost. Give them wisdom where to look and how to help. Make them ministers of Your peace as they care for people in traumatic situations. In Jesus' wonderful name we pray!

*Now, I pray specifically for the Fire Department and volunteers that serves me: _____.

Day 15   Agriculture and Forestry

Exodus: 3:8   So I have come down to deliver them out of the hand of the Egyptians, and to bring them up from that land to a good and large land, to a land flowing with milk and honey.

Deut. 28:8,11-13   "The Lord will command the blessing on you in your storehouses and in all to which you set your hand, and He will bless you in the land which the Lord your God is giving you.... And the Lord will grant you plenty of goods, in the fruit of your body, in the increase of your livestock, and in the produce of your ground, in the land of which the Lord swore to your fathers to give you. The Lord will open to you His good treasure, the heavens, to give the rain to your land in its season, and to bless all the work of your hand.... if you heed the commandments of the Lord your God, which I command you today, and are careful to observe them.

Lev. 26:4   then I will give you rain in its season, the land shall yield its produce, and the trees of the field shall yield their fruit.

Deut. 20:20   Only the trees which you know are not trees for food you may destroy and cut down, ...

2 Timothy 2:6   The hardworking farmer must be first to partake of the crops.

PRAYER:

Lord Jesus, we praise You and thank You that You have brought us into a land flowing with milk and honey. We are honored to lift up our farmers, ranchers and foresters who work diligently to be good stewards of the land. Lord, we stand in the gap for them and ask for

You to cause the splendor of Your majesty to be poured out upon the land and on these servants, who work hard to produce milk, grains, and food for us, and lumber for our homes and projects. Indeed, our breadbasket overflows in this country. In Genesis 1:26 You let man to have dominion over the fish of the sea, over the birds of the air, and over the cattle, and over all the earth ... This is a land where Your glory dwells. You have supplied us with abundant rain, lush fields and amazing forests. Indeed, we grow trees better and faster than anywhere in the world! Give public and private foresters wisdom and good stewardship to supply needs now and for future generations.

Now, we ask that You strengthen and stabilize the markets for our farms and mills. We pray That there would be an abundance of productivity that comes from this land, and that the markets would produce stability and jobs locally for our agricultural and forest industries. You, are Lord of the Harvest!! We thank You for the abundant rainfall that protects us from forest fires and produces supernatural growth rates. We pray for protection over our livestock, crops and forests from the storms of life and from sickness and disease. Protect them in all their ways, Oh Lord! We pray for laws and regulations that support and strengthen our farmers and foresters, and for removal of weighty regulations that are impossible or impractical to meet. Raise up strong men and women who will be overcomers in the faith as they advocate for this cause and give them favor and the ability to communicate when they go before the legislators.

*And now, Lord, I thank You for your abundant provision in my life that I take for granted. Help me to remember those who make it possible, that I might live with food on my table and shelter. I lift up those who produce food and timber or products, and I ask you to specifically bless_____ and encourage them as they produce for us. In Jesus Name! Amen!

Day 16   Fishing and Tourism

Ezekiel 47:9-10   *And it shall be that every living thing that moves, wherever the rivers go, will live. There will be a very great multitude of fish, because these waters go there; for they will be healed, and everything will live wherever the river goes. It shall be that fishermen will stand by it from En Gedi to En Eglaim; (from the top to the bottom of the county); they will be places for spreading their nets. Their fish will be of the same kinds as the fish of the Great Sea, exceedingly many.*

Matt. 6:10   *Your kingdom come. Your will be done, On earth as it is in heaven;*

Isaiah 60   Read this chapter –Proclaim it over our land and people!

PRAYER:

Father, we thank You for the fishing industry in our rivers, bays, and off our coast. You draw people from all over the country to come and enjoy the beauty and refreshing that comes from fishing in our rivers and bays. We pray abundant blessing on all who come, that they would experience a season of refreshing, and they would meet with You. We thank You for our commercial fishermen as well. We ask that You direct and help them, Lord, to find good places to cast their nets. We pray total protection from the heavy machinery and the storms of life. We are grateful, that You are Lord of the harvest. As You multiplied the loaves and the fishes, we ask that You cause our rivers, bays and ocean to be fruitful and multiply. Lord, we do not worship any other than You... we do not worship the sun or the sea...not even the beauty set before us, only You. In Jesus Name!

The Fishing Industry
- Cause the fish of the seas to multiply and be of exceedingly good health
- Give wisdom to the skippers and fishermen for safety, boat management and care
- Bring in the harvest! Strengthen the markets. Build jobs.
- Protection of our fishing fleet from storms. Give Your angels charge over our people and visitors.

Tourism

Thank you, Lord for the beautiful land you have given us to share with visitors. We ask that You create a hospitable environment where Your glory dwells, which attracts visitors to the Presence of God. Let our county be a place of refuge and restoration to all who come. Bring them to worship You and no other, and that they encounter You, here. Help us to welcome tourists with open arms, friendly hearts, pointing the way to Your love. We pray for people who visit to be good stewards of the property where they stay. In Jesus Name we pray! Amen!

Day 17   Homelessness and Poverty

Mark 1:45 *"...so that Jesus could no longer openly enter the city, but was outside in deserted places...."*

Ps 12:5 *"For the oppression of the poor, for the sighing of the needy, now I will arise," says the Lord; "I will set him in the safety for which he yearns."*

PRAYER:

Father, You love Your children. You allowed Jesus to experience the loneliness and discomfort of being homeless. You are a fair and right-eous Father. You hear the struggle and the challenges of those who are poor and bowed down; those who are drug and alcohol addicted; single parents and those who just can't seem to get on their feet. You know us in our innermost being and You know us in our hearts. You know us in our deepest struggles and in our fears and prejudices. You know our pain. We ask that You soften our hearts with wisdom to help solve the problems related to those who are homeless and poor. Some have chosen this lifestyle. We desire to assist those who want to change their circumstances. Give wisdom and discernment to those helping and release resources to help make this transition. Help all of us to love and care more deeply. They are our brothers and sisters, our daughters and our sons. We pray for affordable housing to become available. We pray for those who are transitioning to have a spirit of stewardship and help them to get jobs. Give them favor. Help them with their children. We pray for convicts to find work and to be able to find a peaceable and safe habitation where they can rebuild their lives in holiness. Your love breaks down a multitude of fears. Help our churches to welcome the unlovely and encourage those who are bowed down.

Lord, as I examine my own heart, I ask that You forgive me for harboring resentments and prejudices toward people who do not live or work like I do. Help me to be an overcomer with love toward all Your children. In Jesus Name, Amen

Day 18 Our Veterans, Men and Women of Valor

Joshua 1:14 ... *But You shall pass before your brethren armed, all your mighty men of valor, and help them*

Psalm 20: 8-9 *They have bowed down and fallen; But we have risen and stand upright. 9 Save, Lord! May the King answer us when we call.*

Psalm 44:24-26 *Why do You hide Your face, And forget our affliction and our oppression? For our soul is bowed down to the dust; Our body clings to the ground. Arise for our help, And redeem us for Your mercies' sake.*

PRAYER:

Our faithful Father,

Today, we pray for our mighty men and women of valor who have served our country, bravely and with great courage, who have willingly laid their lives down for our freedoms and to protect the freedom of the world we care for. We thank You, that You know each one and they are precious in Your sight. You know the beginning from the end. You were there in their midst when they were under fire. You weep with those who weep. The battlefield has shifted from a war zone to at home. Thank goodness, You are mighty in battle! You know the battlefield of their minds, especially those who suffer from battlefield fatigue, memories and traumas. You know their deepest fears and wounds. Lord, we ask for the love of the Father to be poured out on our Veterans, especially those who have gone to war, bearing up under impossible conditions, and those who have seen much blood shed. Indeed, Lord, we cry out to You to heal their memories, to heal hearts, quiet fears and restore peace of mind. Lord, what the enemy has intended for evil, You would turn this experience and use it for good. We ask that for those who have endured physical trauma, we ask that You would heal and enlarge resourcefulness. We pray that each Veteran would see Your plan and purpose unfold in their lives. We ask for such complete healing that when they lie down, their sleep is sweet, and their relationships are uncluttered by their traumas. Help our Veterans to draw very near to You, Lord, and to have deep and enduring love in their marriages and for their families. Help these families to cleave together in unity and in faith.

We pray for the marriages and families of our warriors that they would be filled with understanding and encouragement. That You would give them wisdom and endurance to run the race set before them, looking to You, the author and perfecter of their faith. Keep them fixed and stable in the shadow of the Almighty God, drawing each one in tender, healing intimacy. As Your word says in 1 John 4:18, "perfect love casts out fear." Let it be so!

We lift up every Veteran who is struggling with drugs, medications, mental problems, who cannot keep a job or who may not have a family or a home. Lord, our hearts cry out for extra special help for these. Fill their hearts with hope, salvation and strength. For those who desire help, surround them with people and care that will help them get back on their feet. We ask for the resources of heaven, the very present help in times of trouble, just what they need, to come forth. We ask for peaceable habitations for each one and deliverance from these struggles, and for hope to be restored. Help the Body of Christ to rise up and take note, to pray, and to adopt those who are bowed down. In Jesus Name! Amen

Day 19   Businesses and Employment

Colossians 3:22-24   *Bondservants obey in all things your masters according to the flesh, not with eyeservice, as men-pleasers, but in sincerity of heart, fearing God. And whatever you do, do it heartily, as to the Lord and not to men, knowing that from the Lord you will receive the reward of the inheritance; for you serve the Lord Christ.*

PRAYER:

Thank You, Lord for jobs that are available to the people of our county. Thank You that You have given people a mind to work! Fill the workers with an enthusiastic zeal to work with excellence and motivation to serve their employers with gladness. Let all the labor be done with quality, efficiency and honesty. Help our workers give a fair day of work for a fair day of pay! We pray for punctuality, good work habits. Let each worker take pride in doing a good job. We ask for "team effort" and that the work force would be in unity. Melt away pettiness and backbiting in the workplace and let each esteem the others more highly than himself. Let their conduct be decent and in order. Let the supervisors train each employee to the point they succeed. Give great creativity in problem solving. We pray for justice within the workplace and opportunity for advancement based on the merits of skill and experience. Guide our employers and supervisors to be excellent, discerning and encouraging leaders. We pray for new jobs to open up that would allow everyone who wants to work an opportunity to support themselves. Lord, we pray for divine appointments for those who are needing jobs and the employers seeking workers well-suited to their jobs.

*Lord, now I lift up those I know who are struggling with work habits or who need work, and those in need of affordable housing in order to accept offered positions. _____, make their way plain and straight. Show them where to look and give them favor. Let them see You, as an ever-present help in time of trouble. Help me to be a godly encourager and to remember to pray for them until they succeed. In Jesus Name, Amen.

Day 20   Schools, Children, Youth

Proverbs 22:6 *Train up a child in the way he should go, And when he is old he will not depart from it.*

Daniel 1:17 *.... God gave them knowledge and skill in all literature and wisdom; and Daniel had understanding in all visions and dreams.*

PRAYER:

Your Word says we perish without a vision… We ask for an opportunity to restore Christian values and moral standards into the hearts of our children. We ask that You would restore that which was lost throughout our nation--One Nation under God-- including in the classrooms. Let all things be done decently and in order. Help us teach our children to respect and honor authority. We speak life, hope, and peace into our schools and children. Protect our children from the onslaught of the enemy, and pull their interest away from the enemy's camp, and set their hearts on You. Give Your angels charge over our schools and protect them from violence. Uncover, the schemes of the enemy to cause harm, (Drugs, alcohol, promiscuity and deception). Let the passion and power of Your Holy Spirit flow through our schools, bringing peace, righteousness and a climate that is good for learning. Help our children achieve the skills that would allow them to succeed and excel when they complete the work assigned. Build perseverance into our children. Let our children be authors and finishers…. In school and in the faith. We pray You would plant the vision You have for each child and help them to fulfill it. Implant in the children's hearts the knowledge that each one is fearfully and wonderfully made by You, for such a time as this, and that You have wonderful plans for their future if they will persevere. In Jesus Name, Amen!

Now, I pray for our teachers and children. Fill them to overflowing with the ability to connect with each other with delight and to rejoice in achievements. Set their hearts for success! Give our children the ability to sit quietly, to listen carefully, and to apply what they hear. Let the concepts slip into a solid foundation on which they can build. We pray for our children to have early success with reading, writing and arithmetic. And as they achieve, fill their hearts with a hope and a vision. In Jesus Name, Amen!

For all the youth who struggle with bullying, drugs, alcohol, or a poor home life, we ask that You grant them wisdom and strength to come forward to ask for help. Protect them from making decisions that will alter the course of their lives. We pray for the teachers to be able to find and minister to these kids and help them to be authors and finishers in the faith, and in completing school. Give divine wisdom to the teachers and support people to know how to intervene in a timely way.

We Pray for the Christian and Public-School administration, teachers, and support staff that serve our students and community_____

Pre-schools	Community College
Elementary Schools	Colleges and Universities
Junior High/Middle Schools	Sunday Schools
Charter Schools	Youth Groups
Private Schools	Teachers, Administration, Stu-
Home Schoolers	dents

10 Days for My State

Day 21   Government Leaders and Laws

1Tim.2:1-2 *Therefore I exhort first of all that supplications, prayers, intercessions, and giving of thanks be made for all men, for kings and all who are in authority, that we may lead a quiet and peaceable life in all godliness and reverence.*

2 Chronicles 7:14   *If My people who are called by My name will humble themselves, and pray and seek My face, and turn from their wicked ways, then I will hear from heaven, and will forgive their sin and heal their land.*

Jeremiah 29:7   *And seek the peace of the city (state) where I have caused you to be carried away captive, and pray to the Lord for it; for in its peace you will have peace. (paraphrased)*

PRAYER:

Almighty God, whose glory is in the fall of the world, the fountain of wisdom, who's law is truth, and righteous judge of all the earth.

Grant to all of those in administrative authority the wisdom, love, and strength to know You and to do Your will. Fill them with the love of truth and righteousness and make them ever mindful of their calling to serve the people of our great state.

We ask for You to guide and bless our Governor, our state Senators and representatives, our county commissioners, and city counselors that they may enact such laws as shall please You, to the glory of Your name and the welfare of your people. We ask for Your wisdom to find ways to overturn laws which bring defilement to our land. We pray for righteousness and Truth to prevail when these issues are brought to light. Turn our leader's hearts toward You.

We humbly ask You to bless the courts of Justice and the magistrates in all this land; and give to them the spirit of wisdom and understanding, that they may discern the truth, and impartially administer the upright law in the fear of You alone.

O Lord, bless the leaders of our land, that with steadfast purpose they may faithfully serve in their offices to promote the well-being of all people; that we may be at peace among ourselves and be a blessing to other nations of the earth, through Jesus Christ our Lord, who lives and reigns with You and the Holy Spirit, one God, world without end. Amen

*Help me Lord to pray for those who are in authority. Help me to be involved in the process of democracy. Give me Your vision and remind me of Your Word when I vote. Help me to place people in authority who will honor Your precepts. Speak to my heart about how to engage. Do you want me to pray? Do you want me to write letters? I am listening. _____

And now I pray for our State Leaders by name and/or office -

_____

Governor	Treasurer
Lt Governor	State Representatives
Secretary of State	State Senators
Attorney General	All the others that you know of

Day 22   Supreme Court and the Court System

2 Chronicles 19:5-7   Then he set judges in the land throughout all the fortified cities of Judah, city by city, 6 and said to the judges, "Take heed to what you are doing, for you do not judge for man but for the Lord, who is with you in the judgment. 7 Now therefore, let the fear of the Lord be upon you; take care and do it, for there is no iniquity with the Lord our God, no partiality, nor taking of bribes."

Proverbs 8:20; Proverbs 29:4

PRAYER:

Dear Father in Heaven,

We desire to see justice prevail in our state. So, we ask that You guard our court system: The Supreme Court, all the Appellate Courts, Tax Courts, Court of Appeals, Circuit Courts, Municipal Courts and County Courts. May all the Justices take heed to your Word and recognize their awesome responsibility before You. For You traverse the way of righteousness and are in the midst of the paths of justice. We pray You grant these courts wisdom and understanding as they judge righteously. Lord, we ask that You protect our judges from unrighteous influences of our culture and from special interest groups whose purpose it is to undermine and violate Your precepts. We bind our judge's minds and hearts to Your Word, and to the Constitution. We pray Your righteousness to work through and on behalf of our people. We ask that Your Spirit rise up, giving wisdom and discernment to our judges, and that unrighteous decrees would be overthrown in our state and in our nation. Help the people rise up and place judges in positions of authority that will not be swayed by the strongholds of this age. We thank You that our Constitution is based on Your precepts. Now, we commit our judges to rise up, let their 'yes' be "yes," and their 'no' be "no", and they be lined up with the original intent of these biblical precepts. We know that for our land to prosper with laws supporting abortion and laws which undermine your precepts in marriage, family, parental management and education, we need to repent. Justice must prevail; for justice will truly establish our land!

The Supreme Court is the highest court in the State judicial branch. Lord, we lift up each of the Supreme Court justices in our State to You. Have Your way in them, Lord. Help them to hear Your voice as they preside. May they sense Your presence and guidance in all their judgments! In Jesus Name, Amen!

Now, I pray for the Justices of our State Supreme Court and the cases they review _____

Day 23   The Church

John 17:20-22 I do not pray for these alone, but also for those who will believe in Me through their word; that they all may be one, as You, Father, are in Me, and I in You; that they also may be one in Us, that the world may believe that You sent Me. And the glory which You gave Me I have given them, that they may be one just as We are one ~Jesus

Pastor Don addressed the congregation; "They recently did a survey and guess how many churches there are in our state capital?" There was a pause and then one said, "85!" "Nope" answered the pastor. "120?" said another. Wrong again. "200?" Not even close. "How many then?" came the request. Pastor Don quietly answered, "Only one." That's the way Jesus sees His Church, "Only one." Currently there are approximately 4,000 churches in our state. We could never cause everyone to be of "one mind and one accord," but God can. Jesus believed that and prayed His Father would accomplish it. That prayer will be answered. Our duty is to simply agree with that prayer, and pray it ourselves, until it comes to fruition. *(Editor's note – This paragraph can be about any city/state because "Only one" is the only number cited that has any meaning.)*

Ephesians 4:1-4 "I, therefore, the prisoner of the Lord, beseech [pray] you to walk worthy of the calling with which you were called, with all lowliness and gentleness, with longsuffering, bearing with one another in love, endeavoring to keep the unity of the Spirit in the bond of peace. There is one body and one Spirit, just as you were called in one hope of your calling" ~Paul

PRAYER:

OUR THANKSGIVING: "Father God, we thank You for Your many blessings. We thank You for the things that we sometimes take for granted. Thank You for salvation, for the infilling of Your Spirit, and for the truth of Your Scriptures. Thank You for our Pioneer forefathers and mothers, that they came to this land and endured many hardships in order to bring the gospel to this region, and for our ongoing spiritual destiny as a State.

OUR REQUESTS: "Father in Heaven, we humbly ask You to make us one. Help us remember that with all our differences and various interpretations of scripture and mission, we will not always agree, but can be committed to love each other. Help us come together, not around our distinctives, but around Jesus, the Word made flesh, the Preeminent One. Teach us how to honor and serve one another in humility, just as You did while on the earth. Give us grace to take up our cross, lay down our lives, and be an example of Jesus to a world that is still looking for Him. In Jesus strong name, Amen.

OUR DECLARATION: "Father in heaven, we as committed disciples of Jesus, declare to You that the Church of Our State, the collective Body of Christ, will be one unified spiritual body, supplied by the Love of Jesus Christ, in order to witness the love, and power, and testimony of Jesus to a lost and dying world. This we confess by the Lordship of Jesus, to the glory of God the Father, and by the power of the Holy Spirit, Amen."

- Pray for Pastors and Spiritual Leaders to embrace one another as friends.
- Pray for congregations to love and honor one another in spite of distinctives.

- Pray that Jesus will become the center of our worship and the reason for our unity.
- Pray that Churches will be strengthened and have renewed love for the Scriptures.
- Pray for a dramatic increase of His glory/presence among us when we gather together.

In Jesus Name we pray! Amen

Day 24   Our Counties

An Explosion of Intercession Across the State!

Ps. 27:7-8   Hear, O Lord, when I cry with my voice! Have mercy also upon me, and answer me. ⁸ When You said, "Seek My face," My heart said to You, "Your face, Lord, I will seek."

1 Thess. 1:2-3   We give thanks to God always for you all, making mention of you in our prayers, ³ remembering without ceasing your work of faith, labor of love, and patience of hope in our Lord Jesus Christ in the sight of our God and Father

Eph. 6:18   praying always with all prayer and supplication in the Spirit, being watchful to this end with all perseverance and supplication for all the saints—

PRAYER:

Father, thank You for the Body of Christ in all our counties. Awaken them to hear Your voice and respond to Your call, to seek Your face. I lift my voice to You, Lord, to call out for myself and Your Bride to be faithful in following You and Your Word. Thank You, that You know our weaknesses and are merciful to us. Praise You for Your faithfulness to answer our prayers.

We rejoice that You have adopted us into Your family and equipped us to do good works. Thank You for my brothers and sisters across this state who are diligently following You and working together in the "harvest field." Most especially, thank You for showing us Your great, great love and how to love You and others. Thank You for giving us a confident hope in You, that makes an eternal difference, and that it is worth it to give our lives for Your Kingdom.

I lift up my brothers and sisters across this state to You that You will pour out Your grace upon them to keep their love for You strong, to bless every work that You call them to pursue, and to bring them into Your purposes and destiny. Jesus, I personally commit to helping broaden and deepen our unity, so that we will be the answer to Your prayer for us in John 17 to be united like You and the Father are. Thank You for making our unity an effective witness for You and bringing multitudes into Your family!

And now, we lift up organizations like (i.e. Prayer Organizations, State Prayer Networks, National Prayer Networks, Houses of Prayer, Prayer Summits and churches etc.), who are diligently working to develop unity in the Body of Christ and ask for You to give them favor and discernment. Help them find and strengthen the Body of Christ to raise up focused prayer. We ask that You, would release an explosion of intercession across this state and nation. Bring people to their knees, crying out to You for the harvest. Release a passion and a perseverance like we have never before experienced. Do it in me! In Jesus Name, Amen

Day 25   Our People   Part 1

Proverbs 2:1-6   My son, if you receive my words, And treasure my commands within you, [2] So that you incline your ear to wisdom, And apply your heart to understanding; [3] Yes, if you cry out for discernment, And lift up your voice for understanding, [4] If you seek her as silver, And search for her as for hidden treasures; [5] Then you will understand the fear of the Lord, And find the knowledge of God. [6] For the Lord gives wisdom; From His mouth come knowledge and understanding.

PRAYER:

Families: Lord, we lift up the families across our state and ask for Your hand of mercy and truth to be poured out on them. You are our mighty Father, our healer, sustainer and comforter. Our families need Your guidance to know how to raise their children up in the ways of the Lord. Break the generational curses of divorce, addiction, poverty, sexual abuse, perversions of every kind, physical abuse, crime, adultery, hate, and bitterness. Heal the broken hearts of children who have been affected by these traumas. Some of these children have now grown into adults who still carry hurts and pain from a broken past. They need healing. Holy Spirt, bring light to the areas they have attempted to keep hidden in the dark. Bring life to where the enemy has tried to bring death. We also ask for each person to have a redeeming knowledge of Jesus Christ and that each would understand their true identity as a child of the King. We pray scriptural truths over families today, that they will be rooted, grounded and established in who they are in Christ Jesus so that they cannot be shaken and so that chains are broken. They have an inheritance that cannot be taken away. We know that You are faithful to complete a work You started. We speak the truth of who You say we are over our families. We speak life and life abundantly over the families in our communities, state and around the world.

Pregnant Women: Lord, we thank You for every life that You planned before the foundation of the earth. Each life is precious in Your sight. We pray for the mothers, that You would give them wisdom and understanding of Your creative purpose for each life. Fill each woman with a reverence and awe that she is carrying Your baby. Provide these mothers with the support they need to make good and wise decisions. Our hearts are grieved by the numbers of babies being sacrificed by abortion. We pray that You would spring forth an awareness that there are better ways to manage. Draw women who are contemplating abortion to Christian pregnancy centers and put a desire in each woman to complete the pregnancy so that her baby may be raised by loving parents. Give courage to mothers who place babies for adoption, and provide loving, godly, safe homes for each baby. We pray that laws that support abortion are overturned and public reimbursement for this is cut off.

Marriages: Father, we bring the marriages in our state before You. We are troubled by divorce statistics, and that the divorce rate is high even in the body of Christ. We ask You to intervene in the hearts of married couples. Bind up divisions and discouragement and release the unity that comes from You. Give our married couples courage to be truthful, humble and repentant with each other and with You. Cause them to submit to one to another, with pureness of heart and willingness to press through hard times. Be at the center of their relationship. Let them lean on You. Fill them with Your Holy Spirit. When couples struggle, let them know that You are there, Lord. Surround them with godly counselors and friends who can lead, teach and encourage them in the way they should go. Where there is abuse and hatred, we pray for Your wisdom and protection and a way of escape, if needed. Lord may each husband and wife know that they are raised with Christ and that they are to seek those things which are above. May their life be hidden with Christ in You so they may appear with Christ in glory.

Mothers and Fathers: Lord, we thank You for this sacred union which You established when You made Adam and Eve. Lord, help parents love and honor each other the way You love the Church. Let them see the treasure and beauty in a deep relationship between each other with You at the center. Help them to be equally yoked in You. Help them to be rooted and grounded together in You and planted in the Body of Christ. If they do not know You, we ask that You draw them to You. We pray that You would give wisdom, tenderness and kindness to each one. Help them solve problems with kindness. Help them be healed from any ungodly former relationships so they can minister life to one another in purity. Help parents speak words of encouragement and value to one another in front of their children. Help them model the fruits of Your Holy Spirit. We speak peace for marriages. When they are tired, discouraged, distressed, or face life's trials, help them support, encourage and lift each other up. Help them pray together often. Help parents model wisdom and godly behavior to their children. Help them train up their children in the ways they should go so when they are old, they won't depart from it.

Our Children: Lord, we ask that You, would captivate and seal the hearts of our children from a young age. Lead each child by Your Holy Spirit and bring them to a point of repentance and relationship with You through Jesus. Train them up in the way they should go, so when they are old, they should not depart from it. May they know and never question that they are justified by faith and that the blood of Jesus will cleanse them from all sin. May they know they are a child of God. By Your grace may they have peace of mind and increasing faith. May they have rich and transforming fellowship with You and other Christians. We rejoice in the hope of glory as Your love and grace is poured out on their hearts. The Holy Spirit has been given to them and they have been washed, sanctified and justified in the name of Jesus. They are redeemed by Your blood and forgiven of their sins according to the riches of Your grace.

Single: Lord Jesus, I thank You for those whom You have called to be single. We ask that You use them for your glory. Help them be single minded in their pursuit of You. Strengthen them with resolve to stand fast for Your purposes. Give them purity of heart and help them to be very productive in You. Lord, for those who are single for a season, we ask that You would prepare a spouse for them who is like-minded, equipped with passion and resolve for You and that You would arrange divine appointments for them to find the gift of a spouse in due time. Give them patience to keep You the main thing and to not chase after vain imaginations. Let the glory of the Lord be their strength. In Jesus Name, Amen.

Divorced: Father, people are divorced for a variety of reasons. You know each person's heart, their struggles and their desires. Regardless of the cause, we pray for a deep healing to go forth in these people. Draw them to Your throne of grace to find help in times of trouble. Sometimes this is years later. Break ungodly ties and restore what has been lost to each person. Help divorced people live in purity, drawing near to You, Lord. For those who have children, help them speak words of peace to their children regarding their exspouse. Help them strive to live in peace with all people. We bind up wounds of the heart, tormenting spirits and fear. We release healing, hope and strength for their futures. In Jesus Name, Amen.

Day 26   Our People   Part 2

1 Timothy 4:12 *Let no one despise your youth, but be an example to the believers in word, in conduct, in love, in spirit, in faith, in purity.*

Psalm 68:6 *God sets the solitary in families; ...*

Leviticus 19:32 *'You shall rise before the gray headed and honor the presence of an old man and fear your God: I am the Lord.*

PRAYER:

Youth: Let the fire of Your Spirit flood our young people with a vision and a hope throughout this state! Give them holy boldness to follow You and to testify of Your greatness. Make them ministers of Your peace and hope and let a spirit of intercession fall on our young people. Plow up the ground of their hearts and make them a fertile field for the planting of the Lord. Holy Spirit come and speak to the hearts of our youth to keep them pure and holy and unblemished for You. When temptations come near, let Your righteousness rise up and give strength to resist them. Separate each child from corrupt companionship and help them cleave to good friendships that lead to You. Let those who love You have great favor with the multitudes. Make them witnesses to all the earth. We pray that You would impart wisdom to our young people and prepare their hearts to lead the next generation in purity, wisdom and holiness. Raise up righteous young people with servant hearts and leadership skills to be in positions of authority. Let our future generations be as unto You!

Foster Children: Lord, we yoke these children to You, for Your protective care and love, even before they become foster children. Sovereignly fill these children's hearts with Your love and protect them before and after placement. We pray for godly foster homes that will minister love and healing to these children. Father, may they know they have been given the right to become a child of God and may they have every spiritual blessing in heavenly places. Lord, we ask that these precious children know You, the only true God, and Jesus Christ whom You have sent. We pray they would know they are accepted in the Beloved, received by You, adopted by You and complete in You.

Elderly: Lord, at a time in their lives when our elders need You most, make yourself real to them. Fill their hearts with peace. Comfort those who grieve. We pray protection over each one, as they become more frail, that You would uphold them with Your victorious right hand! If they cannot stay at home, we pray that You would go before them and behind them, comfort them as they grieve the loss of independence. Help them to make new friends and prepare the way of the Lord! We pray for every care facility, that You would bring in quality staff who care and protect. The facilities are a mission field, Lord, for the residents and the staff! Let Your name be exalted. Give boldness to those who know You, to lead each other, even the staff, to Your throne of grace. We seal them with Your word. They are created in Your image, You, knew them before You formed them in their mother's womb. Before they were born, they were sanctified and ordained as a prophet to the nations. They are the body of Christ Jesus and a member individually.

Single Parents: Lord, we pray for our single parents. Lord, there are so many of them due to teen pregnancy and divorce. Lord, we do not know what these families have been through, but we cry out that You would be a Father to the fatherless and that You would be an ever-present help in time of trouble. Heal every bit of anger, bitterness or fear. We pray that You would be the "husband" and supplier of resources and strength. Help our single parents to lead their families with wisdom, being faithful to Your word. Help them find You in every situation and circumstance, Lord. We pray for the children of these families to be trained up in the way they should go. Help single parents to administer consistent, wise and godly discipline. Surround these families with godly men and women who encourage and provide them with extended family support. Raise up a standard of protection over the children from un-godly people, motives and influences. When single parents go to court, only You know the Truth of their situation. Turn the heart of the judge to protect the children. Defend the weak and the fatherless; uphold the cause of the poor and the oppressed.

*And now, Lord, I have prayed for many kinds of people whom You love. Open my heart to pray for families or individuals who are struggling. Help me to not be judgmental or critical. Is there an elder, single parent or someone who needs my love and support? I am listening! In Jesus Name! Amen

Day 27   Protection of our Lands

Psalm 93:3-4 *The floods have lifted up, O Lord, the Floods have lifted up their voice; The floods lift up their waves. The Lord on high is mightier than the noise of many waters, Than the mighty waves of the sea.*

Isaiah 43:2   *When you pass through the waters, I will be with you; and through the rivers, they shall not overflow you. ...*

Joel 3:16   *... The heavens and earth will shake; But the Lord will be a shelter for His people. ...*

PRAYER:

Lord, we live in a beautiful state, a land of hills and valleys, forested hills, spacious grasslands and deserts, and many miles of coastline. Lord, first we need to repent for things that You abhor. We ask that You forgive sins that have been committed against our land that cause the ground to cry out. (idol worship, innocent blood shed, immorality of all kinds and broken covenants). We have been a weak and sinful people since the beginning of time, and we are grieved. Wash our land with Your precious blood, and wash us, Lord bringing for-giveness and restoration. We hear the news, filled with anxiety about things that could happen to our land, however, we believe the report of the Lord! We roll every anxiety over on You! We know that when we pray, You, raise up a standard, and that You hear us, so we thank you for this beautiful state which we love. You have given it to be cared for by us, both physically and spiritually. We ask for the out-pouring of Your Spirit, raising up wise stewards over this land.

We ask for your hand of mercy and protection over the fault-line off our coast, and that You would keep the coastlands fixed and stable in the shadow of the Almighty God. Cause tidal waves to dissipate in Your Presence and be as a non-existent thing. The flood waters, they would not overtake us. Have mercy Lord! Lord, in a land soaked with the rains of heaven, we are grateful for the amazing ability You have to send these waters to the sea. Thank you for protecting our land from "over-flowing assaults". We welcome a tidal wave of Your Holy Spirit to flood our land with Your presence and the goodness of the Lord to shake our hearts to depend on You! Lord, there are parts of our nation which are routinely devastated by hail, tornados and hurricanes. Lord, we pray for mercy and protection. Lord, we pray for all the forests, crops and grass lands of this nation. We pray for protection from insects, blights, plagues, and fire. Quench every fiery dart, (anything that would cause harm) that would attempt to ensnare our land. Lord, I ask You to remind me often to intercede for our State that You have given us.

*And now, Lord, I desire to be a wise steward of the land that You have given me in my life. I ask that You reveal to me areas in my life that require more in-depth repentance that cause my ground to cry out; any areas of idolatry, broken covenants, immorality and innocent blood shed. These can be healed when I bring them to Your throne of grace with godly sorrow. Forgive me now for _____, wash me with Your precious blood, fill me with Your Holy Spirit, and cancel the assignment from these things over my life, and the generations to follow. Now I purpose to serve You in freedom from these things. In Jesus Name, Amen

Day 28 Health Care and Health

Jeremiah 33:6 *Behold, I will bring it health and healing; I will heal them and reveal to them the abundance of peace and truth.*

Malachi 4:2 *But to you who fear My name, The Sun of Righteousness shall arise, With healing in His wings; ...*

Luke 9:11

PRAYER:

During this season of immense change in the Health Care Policy and in the Health Care Industry, we ask that You guide national and state legislative leaders of health care with Your wisdom to make good choices on behalf of our people. We ask that the goals of making quality health care affordable and accessible for all our citizens be reached. Keep our health care facilities with Your Mission at the foremost part of their service, and make their way plain and straight, so service can be delivered with a spirit of excellence. Help healthcare facilities to find new and creative ways to reduce the cost of providing care. Keep each of our facilities "fixed and stable" in the shadow of the Almighty God as we go through changes.

Lord, we are grateful to those who give their lives to serve and care for the sick and injured. We ask that You pour out the Spirit of Wisdom upon health workers and caregivers, to be ready in season and out, to do the right thing at a given moment. We ask for Your sovereign touch on all health care workers, to lay hands on the sick, and they shall recover, and be at peace. We lift up _____ **(see memory jogger)**

We pray for God's divine wisdom and healing virtue to be poured out, with quick and accurate diagnosing, appropriate and effective care, and courage and strength to work in the overwhelming challenges of the electronic age and new regulations.

*Lord, You have called me to be an instrument of Your peace and to pray for those who are bowed down and You have given me the authority to intercede powerfully toward anything that exalts itself against Your perfect will. I pray You would give me the boldness and the love to minister life, health, and healing words and prayers for the people around me. Let me impart faith and hope as I do this. Help me to be consistent as I seek Your heart, Lord, asking for help for those going through times of trouble. May You be glorified in all that I do. Lord, I give You my ear to hear, as You help me with my prayer life. I ask You to bring to mind those for whom You would have me pray. _____Listen and pray! In Jesus Name.

Memory Jogger – pray for people in the areas below:
- Federal and State Legislators
- NIH, CDC, HHS, WHO (National Institutes of Health, Centers for Disease Control and Prevention, Department of Health and Human Services, World Health Organization)
- Our Hospitals
- Ambulance Services
- Medical offices, Physicians, PA's, Nurse Practitioners
- Nurses, Therapists, Technicians, CNA's, support Staff
- Chiropractors
- Naturopaths
- Home Health and Hospice Programs
- Dentists, Opticians, Optometrists
- Senior Services to Elderly Disabled & Mentally Disabled
- Nursing Homes, Assisted Living, Foster Homes

Day 29　Electronics/Social Media

Galatians 5:1,16-17 "Stand fast therefore in the liberty by which Christ has made us free, and do not be entangled again with a yoke of bondage." ... [16] "I say then: Walk in the Spirit, and you shall not fulfill the lust of the flesh. [17] For the flesh lusts against the Spirit, and the Spirit against the flesh; and these are contrary to one another, so that you do not do the things that you wish.

PRAYER:

Lord Jesus, how far our culture has come in our ability to communicate and be entertained electronically! We live in an amazing nation that allows freedom of speech. This can be both a blessing and a curse. For the blessing of being able to communicate and do incredible business electronically, we are grateful. But, for the doors we have opened that allow demonic influence, we repent. Father, some have allowed these blessings to become addictive, vehicles of violence, fantasy, and pornography. These tools which can be used for great good can be used for terrible harm: searing consciences, destroying hearts and sacred relationships in our families. In some, these tools have created isolation, fear, loneliness, and often deep darkness. Lord, we are grieved over the things people say or write on electronic devices that they would never say out loud, and for the bullying that is so harmful. We stand in the gap for those who take on an avatar and fantasy identity, and with this do unspeakable acts electronically. This is not who You created them to be. We ask for mercy, Lord. Bring our people to their senses. Draw them away from fantasy and into Your truth. Provide them a way of escape back to reality. Help us minister to and strengthen those who have come under this addictive bondage.

Most Americans, Christians and non-Christians, have been impacted by the electronic god of this age which often consumes our time, energy, and hope. Lord, forgive us for this idolatry that can take over time that could be spent with You or with each other. Lord, we know electronics can accomplish tremendous good: for the spread of the gospel and to help us be productive at work. Lord, take what the enemy has wrought into evil and turn and use it for good. We pray every person would become aware of the snare that electronics can be. Guard our hearts with diligence and self-control. Help us to use this tool with wisdom and purity, and to handle our most precious relationships face to face in love. Help our identity come from You.

Lord, we cry out to You, too, for a nation that has become under the influence of instant gratification. Forgive us and renew a right spirit within us.

Lord, I now examine my own heart, and ask that You would renew a right spirit within me. Forgive me for allowing the god of this age to consume me in these ways: _____. I close the door on these strongholds in my life, now. Lord, give me a Christ-like ability to love my neighbor…as I love myself…Help me to love myself enough that I do not run to fantasy for false relationships. I desire to love those around me face to face, to value them as the person You created, and to communicate my heart with words that bring restoration and hope. Lord, help me to find those who are struggling with electronic addictions, _____(name them) to encourage a way of escape and Lord, if this is me, help me to turn my interest toward You. In Jesus Name

DAY 30   Racism/Bigotry

Matthew 22:36-39   [36] *"Teacher, which is the great commandment in the law?"* [37] *Jesus said to him, "'You shall love the Lord your God with all your heart, with all your soul, and with all your mind.' * [38] *This is the first and great commandment.* [39] *And the second is like it: 'You shall love your neighbor as yourself."*

Galatians 3:28   *There is neither Jew nor Greek, there is neither slave nor free, there is neither male nor female; for you are all one in Christ Jesus.*

PRAYER:

Father, we have been trained up - often according to our culture - and we have adopted beliefs about ourselves and others that violate your most important commandments. Our culture has episodes and roots in historical sin of prejudice, bigotry, violence, and murder against some races, and people groups. Lord, we ask Your forgiveness. We need Your mercy and grace, Your blood to wash us of our national sin. We break the power of this historical sin over the present, and we ask for a sovereign love to take its place. Remove the stain of this sin from our culture and renew a right spirit within our people. Sometimes, bigotry stems from family and cultural values. Sometimes we are completely unaware. We show prejudice and bigotry when we think we are better than another, whether it's race, our sex, obesity, intellect, status, poverty, politics, or religion. Yes - even between churches. We confess this as sin. We are all created by You; called according to Your purpose, Lord, You have called us to love our neighbor as ourselves! This is a tall order. We have thought more highly of ourselves and our own kind than of others. Forgive us as a culture. Break the bonds of wickedness that have wrought these wrong beliefs in us. We are all sinners, saved by grace!

Father, forgive me for beliefs I have harbored in my heart that violate your most precious precepts of loving my neighbor as myself. Now, Lord, examine my heart and bring to my awareness beliefs that I have harbored, hatred that I have justified, and how I have not loved others the way You love me. I need your forgiveness, and I need your help to renew a right spirit within me. Change my heart O God! In Jesus Name Amen

10 Days for Our Nation

Day 31   Pray for Those in Authority

Psalm 33:12 "Blessed is the nation whose God is the Lord". ...

1 Tim.2:1-2 Therefore I exhort first of all that supplications, prayers, intercessions, and giving of thanks be made for all men, for kings and all who are in authority, that we may lead a quiet and peaceable life in all godliness and reverence.

PRAYER:

Lord Jesus, we come to you on behalf of our great nation and ask for your hand of mercy and forgiveness to be extended to us, and to our leadership for we have sinned greatly against You, with many decisions which have made sin legal. We are grieved by this and seek Divine intervention to bring restoration to the laws of our land. We thank You, for those who are willing to serve our nation in a leadership capacity, asking that you bless them with humble, servant-hearted abilities. We ask for Godly and God-fearing leaders who recognize their need to be accountable to You, for each decision that they make, and ask that You would grant them wisdom, knowledge and understanding as they seek You.

We ask for each of our leaders, that you would draw them into the saving knowledge of Jesus Christ, and that you would strengthen and encourage them to stand strong in their faith. Let them practice good moral conduct in all their ways. We pray that they would humbly recognize their inadequacy, and seek Your will through prayer, and let the truth of Your Word burn in their bones such that they cannot contain it. Lord, for those who have wandered away from You, we pray for conviction and repentance. Expose sin and corruption that is hidden in darkness so it can be brought to light. Surround them with Godly counsel and support. Help them be dependable, filled with a heart of excellence and love for You, our people and our nation. Let the Ten Commandments and Your teachings be a filter by which they shape their decisions. We pray blessings over their families and thank them for sacrifices necessary to support leadership. And we pray for the support staff that enable our leaders to make decisions to have the same wisdom, discernment and commitment needed by our decision makers.

Help our leaders respect authority and practice accountability with the American people. Give them courage to reduce heavy tax burdens, regulation and defund un-necessary programs. With the great amount of information placed in our leader's possession, help them to be focused and discerning, resistant to pressure and manipulation, holding Your Word as the measuring stick for decision making. Let them not be swayed by political correctness or fear of man.

For those laws which have gone against Your Word, give our leaders courage to restore righteousness. We pray for them to honor the sanctity of life and to repeal and overturn laws that violate Your will. Make them wise stewards of our national resources and give them a passion to protect the interests of the American people. We pray for unity in our leadership and agreement as they engage in decisions which honor You, and conviction when going against Your will. Lord, Your Word says You turn the hearts of king's whichever way You desire. Turn our leaders back toward You and Your ways.

*Lord, I ask now, to forgive me for not upholding our leaders in prayer regularly. Help me to respect those who are placed in authority and to pray regularly for them. Help me to guard my words, speaking words which edify and strengthen. Lord, rebuild our nation according to Your plan and purposes. In Jesus Name!

I now pray for: Our Federal Government Leaders by name and/or by position or agency _____

Day 32   Restoration of a Nation Divided

Proverbs 14:34   Righteousness exalts a nation, but sin is a reproach to any people.

Psalms 33:12   Blessed is the nation whose God is the Lord, ...

Psalms 133:1, 3   Behold, how good and how pleasant it is for brethren to dwell together in unity! ... For there the Lord commanded the blessing— Life forevermore.

2 Chronicles 7:14, Jeremiah 18:8

PRAYER:

Dear Lord, our heavenly Father,

Our nation is in need of an awakening to Your ways! Your Word says that righteousness will exalt a nation. So, we ask for the hearts of our leaders to be open to your wisdom and ways. We are asking for Your divine intervention to heal our land and that righteous judgments and decisions are made by our government and court system. We ask that honesty and truth would be restored to our culture and very fabric of our society.

Lord, we are grieved by the conduct of our leaders and people as they denounce one another and refuse to work toward the common good of the people. There has been a spirit of division amongst our leaders and people. Your Word says, a nation divided against itself cannot stand. Forgive us Lord! Bring our leaders, regardless of their party, to come together in peace, to work together at re-building the nation we love, to strengthen our infra-structure, to rebuild our military, and to care for our people. Let our leaders and our people put aside their philosophies, pride and pettiness, and seek the higher path of reconciliation. Lord, You, are the Restorer of the breach, and without You, working in each person, we cannot do this. We cry out to You to heal every division and every faction.

We are asking for the unity that is needed to incur Your blessing! Lord, Your Word says that "Blessed is the nation whose God is the Lord." We pray for all those in authority at every level of government – Federal, State and Local. We ask for the Holy Spirit to heal the great division we see in our nation. The clash between Biblical values and ungodly philosophical values, indeed the clash between light and darkness, is a huge reason for this incredible division. But Your Word says, Woe to those who call evil good, and good evil; Who put darkness for light, and light for darkness; but it also says, "I will make darkness light before them, and crooked places straight …For it is God who commanded light to shine out of darkness. These things I will do for them, and not forsake them. Nothing is impossible with You, Lord! So, we pray that there would be a great opening of Your Word in their hearts, that they would be able to experience the joy of salvation. Father, as your people, we purpose to humble ourselves before you and turn from our own selfish ways, that You would forgive our sin and heal our land. We desperately need Your help to do this.

*Lord, if there is any divisive way in me, expose it. I am listening. _____Let the words of my heart and mouth be words of reconciliation and hope. For out of the abundance of my heart, my mouth speaks. Lord, I purpose to build unity and hope in my life, in those around me, in my church and in my country, and especially unity with You. In Jesus name I pray, Amen!

Day 33   The Supreme Court

Isaiah 1:16-17 *"Wash yourselves, make yourselves clean; Remove the evil of your deeds from my sight. Cease to do evil, learn to do good; seek justice; reprove the ruthless, defend the orphan, plead for the widow."*

PRAYER:

Lord, You are a Judicial God, deeply concerned with laws and our human legal system. You are the Lawgiver, the Advocate, and the Judge of the earth; the very foundation of Your throne is righteousness and justice.

- We therefore invite YOUR MANIFEST PRESENCE, O Lord, to the chambers of the U.S. Supreme Court, even now, that no demonic influence would be welcome or able to remain and that angels would stand watch over these men and women.
- We fervently cry out to You for each Justice of the Court and for our Supreme Court as a whole! Remind them of the limits of their authority under the Constitution and restrain them from overstepping that boundary. Help them to judge wisely and humbly.
- Would You pour out a spirit of wisdom and revelation to rest on each of them and that as the book of James tells us, the wisdom from above, not the wisdom from below, would prevail. Thank you that the fear of the Lord is the beginning of wisdom.
- May those Justices who fear You, prepare and rule in the fear of the Lord. "The God of Israel said, the Rock of Israel spoke to me: 'He that rules over men must be just, ruling in the fear of God.' (2 Sam 23:3)
- May the literal fear of God fall upon those Justices who currently do not fear You. "Now therefore, O kings, show discernment; take warning, O judges of the earth. Worship the

77

LORD with reverence and rejoice with trembling." (Ps 2:10–11)

- May the fear of God be upon each member's staff: their clerks, their assistants, their friends, their families and all who influence them.
- May they collectively sense the very power and presence of God hovering over them, warning them of The Lord's righteousness and justice; warning them that they must give an account to the Supreme Judge of the WORLD for their actions.

And now, I pray for our Supreme Court Justices:

We pray for the Godly and righteous replacements of new Supreme Court Justices who would seek Your wisdom and righteousness, and who would prevail with strength and discernment.

Lord, lead us as a nation to wake up and to seek You as our Loving and Caring God, who created us and truly desires to direct us into righteousness and purity. In Jesus Name.

Day 34   The Military / Law Enforcement

Numbers 10:9   When you go to war in your land against the enemy who oppresses you, then you shall sound an alarm with the trumpets, and you will be remembered before the Lord your God, and you will be saved from your enemies.

Deuteronomy 31:6   Be strong and of good courage, do not fear nor be afraid of them; for the Lord your God, He is the One who goes with you. He will not leave you nor forsake you.

PRAYER:

Father, we come to you calling out for the protection of our men and women who are the frontline of battle and for all those troops and families who prepare the way at home. These are our men and women who stand in our nation between us and chaos.

Our nation is in confusion and the value of right and wrong is being questioned with a shift toward tolerance and intolerance. The men and women in Law Enforcement are there to protect ALL lives; black, white, red and yellow; men and women; old and young. All people are precious in Your sight. We pray for Godly wisdom and discernment to be on those who protect our people, to do what is right in Your sight and that their leadership would support this. We pray in Jesus' name for Your hedge of protection over the men and women in Law Enforcement, and for their families for protection in the line of duty, and protection from false accusation based on political correctness.

We pray for both our Law Enforcement and Military to unravel the schemes of the enemy as it pertains to domestic and foreign terrorism. Lord, we ask that you sever the ties of corrupt companionship and bring terrorists to the saving knowledge of Jesus Christ, repenting for their sin and turning from their wicked ways. Provide these new believers a way of escape from the path of darkness and despair. We pray that every terrorist cell would destruct from within, and that they would have utterly failed leadership, failed communication and that every attempt of evil would be thwarted. Expose every scheme and give Law Enforcement insider information, total protection, and success at eradicating those who desire to hurt us.

Father, as our Law Enforcement stand in the gap for our nation, our United States Military stands in the gap against those who come against this great nation from afar. They need Your wisdom and discernment to detect the schemes of the enemy before they arise. We pray in Jesus name for Your protection over these men and women who put their lives on the line for our freedom. We pray that You will give them the insight needed and the boldness to go forth into the enemy's camp. We pray for unity in the Military Leadership, Congress, and the White House: that when the enemy comes in like a flood, we would raise up a standard. Lord, let the United States continue to stand for Liberty for one and all, and when the enemy poured forth murder, and oppression, Our Nation--One Nation Under God--has stood in the gap to re-gain world peace. Lord, let it be so... unless You go into battle before us, we dare not go, for You, oh Lord, are mighty in battle, and You are righteous! In Jesus Name.

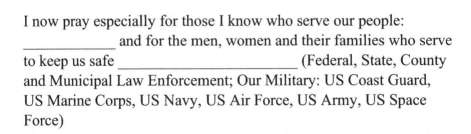

I now pray especially for those I know who serve our people:
_____ and for the men, women and their families who serve to keep us safe _____ (Federal, State, County and Municipal Law Enforcement; Our Military: US Coast Guard, US Marine Corps, US Navy, US Air Force, US Army, US Space Force)

Day 35   The Church

Matthew 16:18 *"... I will build My church, and the gates of Hades shall not prevail against it."*

Ephesians 3:10-11 *"... to the intent that now the manifold wisdom of God might be made known by the church to the principalities and powers in the heavenly places, according to the eternal purpose which He accomplished in Christ Jesus our Lord."*

PRAYER:

Dear Lord Jesus, we come to you believing that you will fulfill Your Word! We know that every Word You have spoken will transform those who believe. Your Word declares that You will build Your church it will be victorious, and all the powers of Hell will not prevail against it! May Your amazing grace flow like a river through our land and the fire of the Holy Spirit ignite your people to share the love that You demonstrated on the cross for us when you gave Your life to save us from destruction!

Father, we have a mandate to share the Gospel and let the light of Jesus shine through us. Help us to realize the urgency and the time we live in and take up our responsibility to pray and seek Your face as never before!

*Dear Jesus, help me to see that I am a part of Your great plan. I must take my place in the army of the Lord and engage in this battle that we will win! Please forgive me for holding back and release me to take my place in great army of the Lord, in Jesus mighty name, amen!

I now pray specifically for:

- Boldness to share the hope that is in me.
- Multitudes to receive Jesus as their Savior.
- Prayer to become a major part of my life.
- A love for the Word of God and His presence.
- Protection from the evil one.
- Joy to fill my life and shine on others.

Day 36   For Christians to Rise Up

Psalm 1:1 "Blessed is the man, who walks not in the counsel of the ungodly, Nor stands in the path of sinners, Nor sits in the seat of the scornful;"

Exodus 18:21 "Moreover you shall select from all the people able men, such as fear God, men of truth, hating covetousness; and place such over them to be rulers of thousands, rulers of hundreds, rulers of fifties, and rulers of tens."

2 Samuel 23:3 "...He who rules over men must be just, ruling in the fear of God."

PRAYER:

Father, we thank You that our founding heritage as a nation is based on faith and trust in You. On our coin and currency are our guiding principles, "In God We Trust". As a nation, we enjoy the privilege, freedom and responsibility to vote as we choose. We thank You, Father, for this God-given liberty. Thank You that we can freely participate in our communities as leaders, run for elected office and that we can exercise our choice at the polls. Let us not take this for granted. Forgive us, Lord, when we have become weak or complacent when it comes to taking a stand for righteousness according to Your word. Lord, we repent and humble ourselves before You. Forgive Christians - who know Your word - for not standing up or voting. Lord, many do not vote consistent with precepts established in Your word. Forgive us for not paying attention to the decay of moral standards that now surround us. We have not only been complacent, but we have allowed the culture to shape our opinions. We have become jaded by media. We have lost sight of Your precepts that were put in place for our safety and protection. Lord, have mercy and grace upon us. Wash us with Your precious blood. Change our hearts, our minds and our faulty thinking. Help us return to the safety of Your Word which we as a nation so desperately need.

Father, we ask for righteousness to rise up in the hearts of Your people. We pray for responsible Christians who will take the time to study issues and learn about candidates who will stand for righteousness as YOU see it. Strengthen Your people with wisdom and discernment to stand up for godly values. Lord, we want to see You as King over our State, as King over the United States. Remind us of our duty to put righteous people into office and to support biblical principles in our culture. Help us place Christian voting guides into the hands of Americans. Help us say, "Yes to Life, No to unnatural death!" We yearn to do what is right in Your sight. Help Christians say, "Here am I, send me!" Raise up godly men and women in leadership roles to re-shape our culture with boldness and goodness. Give them courage and protection. Go before them and grant them favor. In Jesus Name, Amen

Day 37   Community Violence

Ps.55:8-10   *I would hasten my escape from the windy storm and tempest." ⁹ Destroy, O Lord, and divide their tongues, for I have seen violence and strife in the city. ¹⁰ Day and night they go around it on its walls; Iniquity and trouble are also in the midst of it.*

PRAYER:

Father, Your arm is not short! You are righteous and holy. We ask that You capture the hearts of those who do violence and who stir up strife and division. Sometimes this violence is in our homes. Sometimes it is in our communities. Thwart every evil plan and bring their plans to nothing! Bring them to repentance. Deliver each from corrupt companionship. Deliver them from the effect of gangs, drugs, alcohol, rebellion, and hatred and provide them a way of escape. Most of these individuals are people with deep wounds of rejection, fear, and poverty in spirit. It is our heart that You would rescue them from their sin and deliver them from the depths of unrighteousness. So, where sin abounds, grace much more abounds. Lord, the Church needs wisdom and grace to disciple and encourage these people in the way they should go. Make the supporting Christians wise as serpents and gentle as doves. Help us to not grow weary in well doing because in the end we reap a harvest. We dispatch warrior and ministering angels to watch over our cities, neighborhoods, homes and churches to protect them from all harm. Give our police wisdom to uncover schemes hidden in darkness. Protect our police officers from ambushes set against them. Help them follow the leading of Your Holy Spirit.

Lord, I lift up those I know who have fallen into deep rebellion toward You and toward man. _____ (Name them). I pray for a sovereign move upon their heart(s). Help me to pray regularly for them and use me to share Your love. In Jesus Name, Amen

Day 38   Industry and Commerce

Exodus 34:10   And He said: "Behold, I make a covenant. Before all your people I will do marvels such as have not been done in all the earth, nor in any nation; and all the people among whom you are shall see the work of the LORD. For it is an awesome thing that I will do with you.

PRAYER:

Father, I thank You for the incredible gifts and abilities You have given our business leaders and industry to create resources for us and jobs for our people. Lord, we honor the small businesses and mega-companies that sustain our communities and meet big needs. We need each part! Help our companies have the foresight to work together. We pray that those who lead and develop will have vision and creativity that is birthed by You. We thank You for giving them wisdom, vision and passion to solve problems effectively and to efficiently meet needs. We pray for stable and growing markets, and that You equip each company with the ability to think bigger thoughts that bring joy to You. We ask that these businesses thrive so they can provide for current and future employment needs. Lord, help our people to honor and support the hand that feeds them. Lord, we pray for a capable, stable, and honorable workforce. We pray that unnecessary business regulations be lifted. Help each company to regulate themselves uprightly and safely. We pray for unity in the leadership and in the workforce. We bind up mean-spirited competition and corruption and release a common vision and a heart for the welfare of those within their company and those whom they serve. Help them honor You in all they do.

Lord, now, I thank You for the businesses that serve me, for those that make my food, and prepare products that I use every day. Bless and keep safe those who transport all these products so that I may use them. I ask that You help me to be grateful for the many gifts made possible through their hand. Help them in all their ways and help them to thrive. Lead them to You! In Jesus Name, Amen!

Day 39   The Media

Isaiah 61:1-2,4   *The Spirit of the Lord God is upon Me, Because the Lord has anointed Me To preach good tidings to the poor; He has sent Me to heal the brokenhearted, To proclaim liberty to the captives, And the opening of the prison to those who are bound; ² To proclaim the acceptable year of the Lord,... ⁴ And they shall rebuild the old ruins, They shall raise up the former desolations, And they shall repair the ruined cities, The desolations of many generations.*

Philippians 4:8   *...whatever things are true, whatever things are noble, whatever things are just, whatever things are pure, whatever things are lovely, whatever things are of good report, if there is any virtue and if there is anything praiseworthy—meditate on these things.*

PRAYER:

Lord Jesus, we as Americans have immersed ourselves, intentionally or unintentionally, in media of all kinds, unfiltered, untruthful, blasphemous. We are bombarded with demonic imagery wherever we look. Lord, Christians suffer along with non-Christians. We stand in the gap and cry out for an overhaul of our media, and repent for indulging our senses, and for our loss of innocence.

Our nation is in great need of honest communication, that is factual, honorable, and encouraging. We stand in the gap for our networks, social media, and movie making businesses and we ask that You invade all forms of media with Your Holy Spirit. And that You would place in them - those who make decisions - the fear of the Lord (hatred of evil, pride, arrogance, and perverted speech. Place in them, the desire to hunger and thirst for Your righteousness and truth, to be salt and light to a hurting world. Lord, let them shift their mania for creating a story, to that which proclaims hope, healing, liberty, and a raising up of our broken places. Lord, let the words and subjects to which they flock to be filled with truth, nobility, responsibility and righteousness. Let them proclaim and extol the honorable and minimize coverage of ill repute and darkness. Indeed, our media has the ability to exalt or tear down a culture, so cause a shift in cultural values of our people to be drawn to light. Help our media leaders to take this responsibility seriously. Help Americans to flee wickedness in their media choices. Expose media that is hidden in darkness and cause the market on this kind of media to dry up. Bring healing to those who are bound by pornography, immorality of every kind, violence, and treachery. Help the American people to choose salt and light in their programming choices and to flee from soaking in ungodly media.

*Now, Lord, I ask that You examine my heart, and bring conviction when I entertain myself with demonic /un-Godly imagery. Lord, make me aware now, of programs I need to avoid _____. I confess this as sin. Fill my heart with a hunger for what You say is righteous. In Jesus' name, Amen.

Day 40   Addictions

Titus 2:12 *"teaching us that, denying ungodliness and worldly lusts, we should live soberly, righteously, and godly in the present age,"*

1 Peter 5:10 *But may the God of all grace, who called us to His eternal glory by Christ Jesus, after you have suffered a while, perfect, establish, strengthen, and settle you.*

In the United States, the opioid epidemic kills 130 people each day and costs the U.S. economy $78 billion a year.   There are now more people seeking treatment for opiate addiction than alcohol addiction. Eighty percent of people on heroin were on prescription pain killers. Although pain killer prescriptions are dropping, heroin use has climbed. An estimated 88,000 alcohol related deaths occurred during 2019. *

PRAYER:

Father, we humbly come before You to find help in time of trouble for people who struggle with drug and alcohol dependency. This is devastating for the addicted and for their families. We cry out asking You to bring a wave of deliverance that sets free those with addictions. Break this stronghold over my city, county, state. and nation.   In Jesus' Name, loose the bondage and bring freedom to the captives. Speak hope to the hopeless. Make them more than conquerors. Father, we lift up families and children who are caught up in this struggle with an addicted family member.   Bind the spirit of anger, lying, chaos, suicide, and drama that often accompanies addictions. We ask for redemption and restoration of the addicted and their families. Heal their hearts. Help them learn to live in freedom. Draw them to Your throne of grace. Help us love these struggling people and their families and give us Divine boldness and love to facilitate getting them into treatment and safety. Lord, You are the Way, the Truth and the Life. You, Lord, are where their help comes from. We pray for a release of the gifts of Your Holy Spirit: Love, joy, peace, patience, kindness, goodness, faithfulness, gentleness and self-control.

We ask that You assist our federal, state and local law enforcement to ferret out drug trafficking. We beseech You, Lord, to break the power of the drug cartels which manufacture and ship drugs into our country. Give protection, wisdom and strength to our law enforcement who deal with drug interdiction. We pray that federal and state agencies would have wisdom and the policies in place to identify and eradicate prescription and illegal drug abuse.

Lord, I ask for healing in my own life from any kind of addiction that has held me in bondage. I ask for strength to seek the help and guidance I need for myself or my family. Give me courage to face these giants in my life. Heal my heart and make me whole. Lord, I have had people in my life who have hurt me emotionally (and possibly physically and sexually) when they have been "under the influence". Name the hurts _____. Now, Lord, I choose to let the pain of my past be healed. Give me the grace to forgive _____ (Name) for these wounds. What they did was wrong, but bitterness holds me in captivity. I forgive _____ (Name) for sins against me. Lord, I have hated myself in this situation. I ask You to forgive me for not honoring the gift of life which You have given me and for my self-hatred and shame. Thank you for healing me of self-hatred and shame. I invite You, Lord Jesus, to fill the place with Your peace which bitterness and wounding had occupied. Speak to me. I am Your child. (Listen). I thank You for freedom. In Jesus Name, Amen.

*data taken from: https://usafacts.org/articles/opioid-addiction-deaths-and-treatment-latest-analysis-data/ , May 2019.

10 Days for the World

Day 41   The Peace of Jerusalem

Psalms 122:6-7 *"Pray for the peace of Jerusalem: "May they prosper who love you. Peace be within your walls, Prosperity within your palaces."*

Genesis 12:3 *I will bless those who bless you, And I will curse him who curses you; And in you all the families of the earth shall be blessed."*

PRAYER:

Dear Lord Jesus, thank you for your faithfulness! We pray for Jerusalem to experience the peace of God that passes all understanding! Thank You for Your undying love for Your people and for Your land. Thank You for Your people in this land, that there is a living, growing body of the Messiah in Israel, that Jewish people are having their eyes opened to who their Messiah is and some are receiving Him. Lord, we are looking forward to when You will lift the veil fully from the eyes of the Jewish people which has been and is preventing most from recognizing You. Prepare the hearts of Your people to see clearly who You are. We have heard that there are many rabbis who have secretly accepted Yeshua. When will it be Your time for them to reveal themselves? Let it be so, Lord! May Israel look to You for their salvation rather than putting their trust in government or in the Israeli Defense Force or in religious leaders or practices.

As Christians, we understand the biblical significance of Israel. The nations of this earth need to support and stand with Israel. We have to understand that Israel is fighting our battle, because the enemies against Israel are against us too. The battle waged against Israel is a spiritual battle as much as a battle with guns and military and we need to be in prayer. Father we pray that the leaders of the nations will have a biblical understanding of Genesis 12:3 – that those who stand with Israel will be blessed and those who oppose Israel will find themselves an adversary of God.

Lord, we thank You for the establishment of Jerusalem as the rightful capital of Israel and ask that You would move on the hearts of other nations to uphold her and stand beside her in support. We thank You that our United States of America has taken a stand to do this.

Therefore Father, help me to understand and pray for the peace of Jerusalem and the relationship between the Nations of the earth and Israel. I know that You want the best for Israel and will always watch over that land of your choosing. In Jesus' great Name, Amen!

I now pray specifically:
- That the Palestinians would recognize that Israel has a right to exist.
- For Israel's strength and resolve in the face of imminent threats from Iran, and the threats of missile attacks on its borders.
- Quench every fiery dart
- Let every curse or assignment from the enemy, fall as dust to the ground and would not light.
- That the anti-Semitism in the world and especially on campuses of our universities would end.
- As a Christian, help me to support those whom you support, Lord, and to bless those whom you bless. Mighty God, bring your salvation to Israel.

- Bring your salvation to the whole earth. In Jesus Name, Amen!

Day 42   For the Poor, the Hungry and Downtrodden

Deuteronomy 15:11   *For the poor will never cease from the land; therefore, I command you, saying, 'You shall open your hand wide to your brother, to your poor and your needy, in your land.'*

1 John: 3:16-18   *16 By this we know love, because He laid down His life for us. And we also ought to lay down our lives for the brethren. 17 But whoever has this world's goods, and sees his brother in need, and shuts up his heart from him, how does the love of God abide in him? 18 My little children, let us not love in word or in tongue, but in deed and in truth.*

PRAYER:

We pray today for God's people, His creation. We pray that we, as humanity might identify with our human face. We pray for our world divided. God of life, into your world You come. Into this divided human community, You arrive. You sit amongst the poor, but the wealthy do not see You. You, walk with the lonely and the abandoned, but those with power cannot hear Your footsteps. You, stand among the hungry crowds awaiting food, but the greedy will not share their food with You. You live among the powerless, the frightened and the weak, but the corrupt fail to notice and continue to exploit You. God of hope deliver us all from self-righteousness so that while we may call the world towards a different way, we might also become the answer to the prayers of the silent, suffering, and struggling ones. God of justice grant us the courage to live as well as proclaim Your gospel. God of life grant us the energy to serve others in Your name. God of love, enable and allow us, with all our weaknesses and fears, to continue this walk of faith, for faith and in faith.

O God, we identify now with those who lack food. Give us (the world) this day, our daily bread. Bring to our awareness those in need. Move on our hearts to share with those who have not, and to weep for those who are downtrodden. We pray for people in war torn countries where corruption has caused control of the food. We pray that You would raise up angels over those, bringing food and blankets. Give favor to those supporting the people and make a way where there hasn't been a way to supply needed assistance. Show the helping organizations how to get the food to the right places. Give helping organizations discernment on who and how to help, and to recognize true need. Help us to supply generously to those who are helping, (like World Vision, Samaritan's Purse and others). God, the hungry and the not hungry stand as one before You; loved with the same love, both in need of You and each other. Lord, rescue Your children; fill their stomachs with food and their hearts with gladness and hope, so that they, too, might experience the luxury of dealing only with their spiritual hunger, their emotional hunger and their psychological hunger. Send your Spirit to all of us, until we all feast with Jesus in the age to come.

And now, I submit my heart and my resources to You, Lord. Speak to me about how You want me to help. Who would You like me to pray for? How can I help…could it be my neighbor? How can I give? I am listening. In the Name of Jesus, we pray. Amen.

Day 43   For the Outpouring of the Holy Spirit Upon the Nations of the Earth

Matt 7:7-8 Ask, and it will be given to you; seek, and you will find; knock, and it will be opened to you. [8] For everyone who asks receives, and he who seeks finds, and to him who knocks it will be opened.

James 4:8; Jeremiah 29:13; Acts 2:17, Matt. 5:6, Jeremiah 33:3

PRAYER:

O Lord...We come, so hungry & thirsty for a move of God. We long to see a fresh, dynamic outpouring of the Holy Spirit across every Nation. O God awaken the heart and soul of every man, woman and child. May there be a desperate longing to know You, Jesus, and experience an outpouring of Your Holy Spirit in the midst of everyday life. In all Your splendor of Your Holiness, draw the Bride of Christ deeper—deeper into the realms of Your perfect love. May our hearts have a burning desire to experience the richness and the fullness of Your Glorious presence. Blessed are those who hunger and thirst for righteousness, for they will be filled.

Open our spiritual eyes and ears and give us an eagerness to heed the call to pray and seek Your face, to know the very heartbeat of our God. Set our hearts ablaze with a deep seeded passion to love You more! Speak to us Lord, comfort, train and teach us to walk in Your ways so that we will not be conformed to this world! Let our hearts hunger and thirst for your righteousness and be filled with delight day after day, as we continue to rejoice in Your magnificent love.

Lord, draw us into Your Holy Word and teach us to linger at Your feet, for there we will come to know the deep seeded Truth and hidden secrets of the Lord. "Call to me and I will answer you and will tell you great and hidden things that you have not known."

We ask for a dynamic outpouring of the Holy Spirit that this world has never witnessed before! O King of Glory hear the cry of our hearts.... Draw us nearer, nearer O Lord.... And may the whole world come running to YOU!

*And now, Lord, I personally come into Your presence and worship You. I invite You, Holy Spirit to teach my heart and speak Your wisdom to me. I want You to be my comforter and guide. Give me ears to hear Your voice, and the voice of a stranger I will not follow. Speak to me through Your Word, through wise counsel, through nudging's to do something. Make me aware of Your still small voice. The voice of God, the Creator of the whole universe, funneling Your whispers of intimacy and wisdom into my heart. I am awed by Your love. Help me to worship You without abandon until I sense Your presence. Strengthen my resolve to serve you fervently, every day. I do this now.... Come, Holy Spirit, Come! I welcome You! In Jesus Name

Day 44   For Missionaries

Revelation 14:6-7   *Then I saw another angel flying in the midst of heaven, having the everlasting gospel to preach to those who dwell on the earth—to every nation, tribe, tongue, and people— 7 saying with Pa loud voice, "Fear God and give glory to Him, for the hour of His judgment has come; and worship Him who made heaven and earth, the sea and springs of water."*

PRAYER:

Father, we thank you for the amazing men and women whom You have called to reach every tongue, tribe and every nation in the whole earth. As we pray for all missionaries, we also pray for missionaries that we know or support, _____, that all will be filled with the Holy Spirit and will daily walk in His power and that they will speak the Word of God with boldness. Grant them Your specific direction for their ministries. Help them to present the gospel clearly to unbelievers, and for You to prepare the hearts of those preparing to hear the Word. Let them be vessels through which Your love can flow. We pray that You would grant them great favor and they would be accepted by the people, believers and missionaries in the area where they are laboring. We pray for divine appointments, being in the right place at the right time, with the right resources and that their ministries would be exceedingly fruitful and multiply, and that You would glorify Yourself through them. We pray for organizational skills and the ability to prioritize and discern projects and that You would bless them in all that they do. Let them be authors and finishers in the faith as You direct.

Lord, we pray that You will protect them from the attacks of Satan and his demons. Deliver them from loneliness, discouragement and frustration. It is our heart that You would deliver them from the hand of the enemy, however, we thank You that You are an ever-present help in times of trouble, and if persecution takes place, we plead that each missionary will endure persecution in a Christ-like manner and will be willing to give his/her life for the gospel's sake if that is what is called for. We pray for the families of our missionaries that they be strong and of good courage, filled with a common vision and passion. Lord, I ask that You to bless and strengthen missionary families. We pray especially for missionary children, for Your love to encompass them round about, and that You would help them with hearts of obedience, passion for the local outreach and godly friends. Thank you for family unity and for servant hearts. We pray You would give peace and assurance about the care of their family members that are left at home. Father, I plead that You will continually protect them from all harm and ask that You would strengthen them spiritually, emotionally, physically and as a family.

We pray for abundant provision, and that You would raise up prayer partners, finances, and support that is needed of every kind. That there is no lack, in fact that You would mobilize the resources of heaven, even the cattle on a thousand hills to come forth to meet needs. Thank You, that You supply more than enough!

*And now, Lord, I ask that You help me to pray regularly for our missionaries and their families. Examine my heart and speak to me about my involvement with missions. Show me how You would like me to be involved supporting the laborers in the mission field, or are you calling me to go? Do you want me to increase my giving? I am listening! In Jesus Name! Amen!

Day 45   Widows and Orphans

James 1:27   Pure and undefiled religion before God and the Father is this: to visit orphans and widows in their trouble, and to keep oneself unspotted from the world.

Deuteronomy 14:29   ...and the fatherless and the widow who are within your gates, may come and eat and be satisfied, that the Lord your God may bless you in all the work of your hand which you do.

Psalm 68:5-6   A father of the fatherless, a defender of widows, Is God in His holy habitation. ⁶ God sets the solitary in families; ...

PRAYER:

Lord, help us to identify with humanity when we are far removed. It's hard to imagine the circumstances of many of these people. It's difficult to ascertain the uncertainties, difficulties, and hardships they face every day, or the loneliness they feel. Many are vulnerable. Father, we pray for widows and orphans throughout the world. We ask that You, in your great mercy and grace, would meet and heal their physical, emotional, and spiritual needs in a powerful, evident way. We pray for their salvation, if they don't know You, as Jesus prayed that, "they may know You, the only true God, and Jesus Christ whom Thou hast sent."

Father, we ask that you bring godly believers into their lives to be ministers of love and good works, full of humility, compassion, and encouragement, to teach them about You, to bless their lives in practical, needed ways. And that these laborers would not grow weary in doing good but would sense Your favor and equipping. Draw widows and orphans close to You in deep and trusting ways. Replace despair with hope. Replace fears with assurance. Give them physical strength, food, shelter, emotional support and spiritual sustenance. Keep them in your perfect peace. Let them clearly see and acknowledge You at work in their lives. Fill their hearts with reverence, repentance, hope, and trust in You. Help them to turn to You, to petition You in all of their ways. Fill them with Your wisdom. Give them an eternal perspective. Give them a stronger faith, belief and trust in You and a deep assurance of knowing that You are always with them. Lord, we lift up the agencies that minister to populations of widows and orphans and ask for favor from the host countries to let helping agencies in. Help them to find the people who need help most. Lord, we pray that children who need homes and protection would be placed with loving, safe families. We lift up the children who are sold into slavery or human trafficking to be delivered sovereignly into protection. We pray for their healing.

*Lord, open my eyes to see what I, where I am, can do for them. And now, I lift up widows, children who may be in foster care, children of single parents who may need my love and support. Remind me Lord to actually DO to others as I would want done for me. What can I do that might ease the burden? Lord, do You have someone in mind? _____I am listening. In Jesus' name I pray. Amen.

Day 46   The Persecuted Church

Jeremiah 20:11   But the Lord is with me as a mighty, awesome One. Therefore my persecutors will stumble, and will not prevail. They will be greatly ashamed, for they will not prosper. Their everlasting confusion will never be forgotten.

Psalm 9:13 John 15:18 & 20 Romans 8:35

PRAYER:

Sovereign God, we worship You and we acknowledge that You know all of those who suffer in Your name. We remember those who are imprisoned for their faith and ask that they would join with the Apostle Paul to see that even though they remain captive, their chains have furthered the gospel, not frustrated it. May they inspire and embolden their fellow believers to speak the word of God more courageously and fearlessly.

God of all comfort, for those who are tortured both in body and mind, give them the grace to endure and to see their suffering as part of following in Christ's footsteps. Merciful God, for those asked to pay the ultimate price; may they truly know Christ and the power of His resurrection and the fellowship of sharing in His sufferings, becoming like Him in His death.

Father God, for those who are widowed and orphaned may they know the comfort that comes from Your promised presence even when they walk through the valley. May they be strengthened by Your Spirit, enabling them to rejoice with the psalmist as they proclaim that the Lord will not abandon them in death.

Heavenly Father, we ask that You make us ever mindful of our brothers and sisters around the world who need us to stand with them as they suffer in Your name. Teach us what it means to overcome by the blood of the Lamb and by the word of our testimony; we pray that we would not love our lives so much as to shrink from death.

O Lord hear our prayer. Lord have mercy on our brothers and sisters in Christ, may we be aware of the situation they are facing and to never forget them in prayer, or in any other way we can be of help to them. May You send them angels from heaven to comfort them and assure them of Your constant care and love!!

*And now, Lord, in my own life and faith, help me to endure persecution with faith and grace. Help my soft answers to turn away wrath. Help me to be strong and of good courage. Help me to bless and pray for my persecutors and for those I know who are undergoing persecution. Let me not shrink away in fear, but let me face my persecutors with gentleness, courage, and even love. In the Name of Jesus Christ, we pray. Amen

Day 47   Protection From Evil

Romans 8:37-39 ... we are more than conquerors through Him who loved us. ³⁸ For I am persuaded that neither death nor life, nor angels nor principalities nor powers, nor things present nor things to come, ³⁹ nor height nor depth, nor any other created thing, shall be able to separate us from the love of God which is in Christ Jesus our Lord.

2 Timothy 1:7; Psalm 91:1-16; Psalm 27:1

PRAYER:

O Lord, as we walk in the midst of troubled times, shield, protect and strengthen the Body of Christ throughout the world from the evil one. Let our faith arise even in the midst of all the turmoil! For You have not given us a spirit of fear, but of power and of love and of a sound mind....You, promise to never leave us nor forsake us. Therefore, when darkness surrounds us, let us boldly confess "The Lord is My Helper; whom shall I fear?" Lord we look to You...A Strong Tower of Refuge, Our Rock; Our Shield, and the Horn of our Salvation, Our Savior...Our Deliverer...You are the Resurrection of Life! You are our Hiding Place; You preserve us from trouble; and surround us with songs of deliverance. Remind us Lord that we as humans are no match for the enemy...our help must come from the Lord! Therefore, when darkness surrounds us, let us be quick to call upon the name of the Lord...Our Defender...Our protection...Our Faithful God, in whom we trust!

May the Body of Christ hear Your call to prepare for battle...To arise to their rightful place with a dynamic holy boldness! May we stand firm on the Holy Word as we face adversity and not fear the terror of night, nor the arrow that flies by day, nor the pestilence that stalks in the darkness, nor the plague that destroys at midday...!! O God empower your people to be strong in the Lord, and fully trust Your Holy Word...For you have provided the weapons to demolish strongholds through Your word and the spirit-empowered prayer! Remind us to daily put on the whole armor of God, that we may be able to stand against the devil's schemes...for we know we wrestle not against flesh and blood,....Therefore, prompt us to put on the full armor of God, so that when the day of evil comes, we may be able to stand our ground, praying for one another!

Thank you for your mighty protection, Lord...For who shall separate us from the love of Christ? Shall trouble or hardship or persecution or famine or nakedness or danger or sword? As it is written, "...We are more than conquerors through Him who loved us...nothing will be able to separate us from the love of God that is in Christ Jesus our Lord."

Lord may our Brothers and Sisters in Christ seek you with all their hearts and be filled to overflowing with the Light of Your Presence!! Help us NOT be afraid to love and encourage others, even in the midst of dark times.

Bless the Lord O my soul.... For You never sleep nor slumber... You are constantly watching and caring for Your people! — Keeping us from all harm— You will forever keep guard over our lives...our coming and going, both now and forevermore. With God as our Defender.... who can be against us?

*And now, Lord, I submit areas of my life to You that cause me fear and anxiety, and I repent for entertaining them. I confess them as faithlessness. They are _____. You have given me Your Word to overcome ALL the power of the evil one, even in my own mind. Today, I lay my fears at Your throne of grace. Help me to walk free from these and leave them with You. Fill me with Your Holy Spirit and Faith to walk boldly and in victory over ALL these things. In Jesus Name! Amen!

Day 48   Wars and Rumors of Wars

Matthew 24:6   And you will hear of wars and rumors of wars. See that you are not troubled; for all these things must come to pass, but the end is not yet.

Isaiah 16:3-5; Psalm 91

PRAYER:

Lord, we thank you that You are Lord over all the Earth and that Your ways are higher than our ways. Our hearts grieve when we hear about tribe against tribe, and nation against nation. And our hearts are heavy when our nation is at war. But we stand with You, Lord God Almighty, and we pray that the nations will bow their knees to You and hear Your voice. We pray the nations of the earth will rise up in righteousness to bring liberty to the captives and peace to war torn lands. We grieve over evil rulers in the world and the demonic influence that causes hate, discontent, and domination. As we read Your Word, we know that throughout the ages there have been evil kings and good kings. What made a good king was that they loved and honored You. The evil kings worshiped other gods, greedy and oppressed their people. Lord, we stand in the gap for those tribes and nations who are at war, and we pray for wisdom and godliness to arise. That You would overcome great darkness with divine light. That You would cause goodness and mercy to prevail.

We pray for people groups, families and individuals who attempt to escape war torn areas and persecution. Provide them a way of escape. We ask that You would be with them, and that You would lead them into all understanding of Your divine grace and mercy, and especially that you would push back the forces of darkness that have caused blindness to the gospel, and open the Kingdom of heaven to every refugee, bringing hope, salvation, and restoration. We pray for families to be re-united. We pray for protection from abuse, hunger, and disease, and for adequate housing. We pray for protection and deliverance from exploitation and from human trafficking. Expose things hidden in darkness for the protection of all the refugees and the helpers and deliver them from the hand of the evil one. We ask that You prepare the way and remove red tape for godly organizations who will bring the help and resources required for day to day, but also that they would bring a powerful gospel message that would touch the hearts of refugees. We pray for absolute revival to run like wild-fire through refugee camps, and they would become places of discipleship, hope and strength. We pray for those ministering in refugee camps that You would protect and prepare them to minister the gospel powerfully to those in need. We pray for signs and wonders and miracles to be released in a mighty move of God. We pray for removal of godless leaders where tyranny, corruption and oppression have prevailed. Have mercy, Lord. Bring restoration. Turn the hearts of kings toward You and restore righteousness.

*And now Lord, what country would You like me to pray for, and how would You like me to pray. I am listening _____. In Jesus Name, Amen.

Day 49   Strengthen the Body of Christ

Isaiah 61:1-3   The Spirit of the Lord God is upon Me, Because the Lord has anointed Me To preach good tidings to the poor; He has sent Me to heal the brokenhearted, To proclaim liberty to the captives, And the opening of the prison to those who are bound; ² To proclaim the acceptable year of the Lord, And the day of vengeance of our God; To comfort all who mourn, ³ To console those who mourn in Zion, To give them beauty for ashes, The oil of joy for mourning, The garment of praise for the spirit of heaviness; That they may be called trees of righteousness, The planting of the Lord, that He may be glorified.

Ephesians 3:15-20; Colossians 1:9-11; Isaiah 58:6-7; Isaiah 1:17; Hebrews 13:21

PRAYER:

Lord, we lift up the Body of Christ around the world and pray that out of Your glorious riches she may be strengthened with power from on High. We pray for each church corporately and individually, and each Christian, to be rooted and established in love. May we begin to grasp how wide, how long, how high and deep is the love of Christ, a love that surpasses all knowledge. May our churches and people be filled with wisdom, guidance and understanding, so that we may live lives worthy of the Lord. May we be pleasing to You in every way: bearing fruit in every good work, growing in Truth and the knowledge of God. Let us stand solidly upon your Holy Word, for it is right and true and let us never stop praying for one another!

Lord, let the churches of the earth be filled with strength, endurance, and patience with a heart filled with love, understanding and encouragement. Help us to live in complete harmony with each other and

111

always be ready to be a father to the fatherless, a defender of widows, feed the hungry and clothe those in need. May we shine the Light of Life into the darkened world, preaching the Good news to the poor; bind up the brokenhearted, and proclaim freedom to the captives; release prisoners from darkness and comfort those who mourn. May we be faithful to Shepard our flocks, work our fields and vineyards.... Oh, that we may be called Oaks of righteousness displaying Your Splendor!

O God instruct the churches and your people and teach us in the way we should go. Gently guide us with Your eye. May Your Word be a lamp unto our feet and a light unto our path. Faithfully equip us Lord, with every good thing needed for doing Your will. We surrender our hearts...Do Your work in us, preparing us for what is pleasing to You.

Now to Him who is able to do immeasurably more than all we ask or imagine, according to His power that is at work within the churches throughout the earth and in our own heart, to Christ Jesus be all glory and Honor...throughout all generations for ever more! Amen.

Day 50   Growth of the Church

Matt 28:18-20   And Jesus came and spoke to them, saying, "All authority has been given to Me in heaven and on earth. [19] Go therefore and make disciples of all the nations, baptizing them in the name of the Father and of the Son and of the Holy Spirit, [20] teaching them to observe all things that I have commanded you; and lo, I am with you always, even to the end of the age." Amen.

2 Peter 3:9   The Lord is not slack concerning His promise, as some count slackness, but is longsuffering toward us, not willing that any should perish but that all should come to repentance.

Matthew 24:14   And this gospel of the kingdom will be preached in all the world as a witness to all the nations, and then the end will come.

Joel 2:16, Mark 16:15, Acts 16:5 2 Timothy 1:7-9

PRAYER:

Lord, we cry out to You to gather the people, sanctify the congregation, assemble the elders, gather the children and nursing babes; Let the bridegroom go out from his chamber, and the bride from her dressing room. Your Word is clear that You are not willing that any would perish. Your mission field is the whole earth. Father, we ask that You fill the earth with the groaning that calls for You, for the infilling of Your Holy Spirit, for the call to repentance, salvation and the healing of the people of the whole earth. We are commanded to go to all the world to preach the gospel to every creature and bring in the lost. We pray for new believers to believe, be baptized and discipled and to be added daily to the Church. They shall ask the way to Church, with

113

their faces toward it saying, "Come and let us join ourselves to the Lord in a perpetual covenant that will not be forgotten."

We ask that You draw believers together in every land, protect them, fill them full of Your truth, make them disciples, keep them fixed and stable and prepared to preach the gospel. Lord, You, rejoice over every lost person being found. We thank You, that You never leave nor forsake us, but Lord, if we wander, please come after us! We are added to the Body of Christ, one heart at a time. We pray for our hearts to be yoked to You, hungering for Your word, and seeking to be under the authority and care of the fellowship of believers. Help us to seek life giving and Spirit inspired teaching…indeed a planting of the Lord! Let Believers be trained up in the way they should go so that when they are mature, they won't depart from it. Lord, grow Your Church, make us Your pure, spotless and unblemished bride. We see with anticipation …behold, a great multitude which no one could number, of all nations, tribes, peoples, and tongues, standing before the throne and before the Lamb, clothed with white robes, with palm branches in their hands.

*Lord, I am Your disciple, and You speak to me to preach the gospel to the world around me. Teach me how to love and share Your Word, your truth. I repent for any timid-ness in sharing Your love and Word, For God has not given me a spirit of fear, but of power and of love and of a sound mind. Help me to go the extra mile and bring Your children home to You. In Jesus Name, Amen!

Made in the USA
Middletown, DE
16 February 2022

61289348R00066